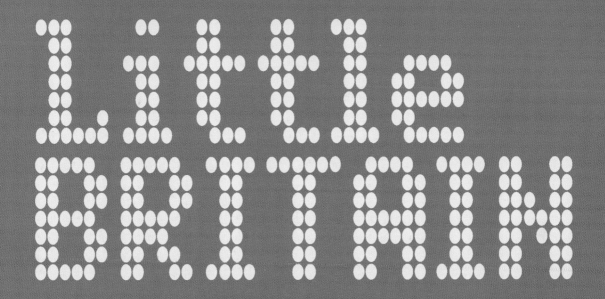

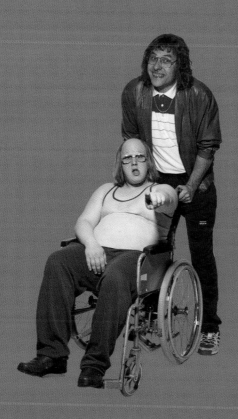

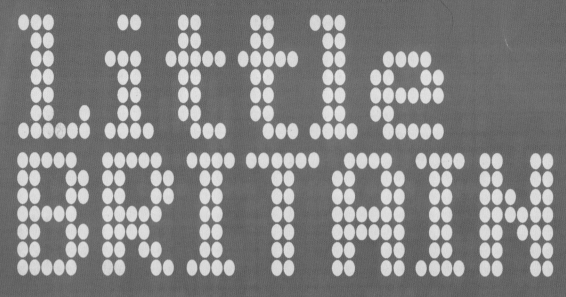

Little BRITAIN

Written by
MATT LUCAS
AND
DAVID WALLIAMS

HarperCollins*Publishers*

Britain, Britain, Britain. The land that gave the world so much. Mad cow disease, happy slapping and Sky One's Dream Team. But who are what live here, sir? Come with me, as we meet the inhabitants of Little Britain. Do you really like it? Is it is it wicked? We're lovin' it, lovin' it, lovin' it. **We're lovin' it like that!**

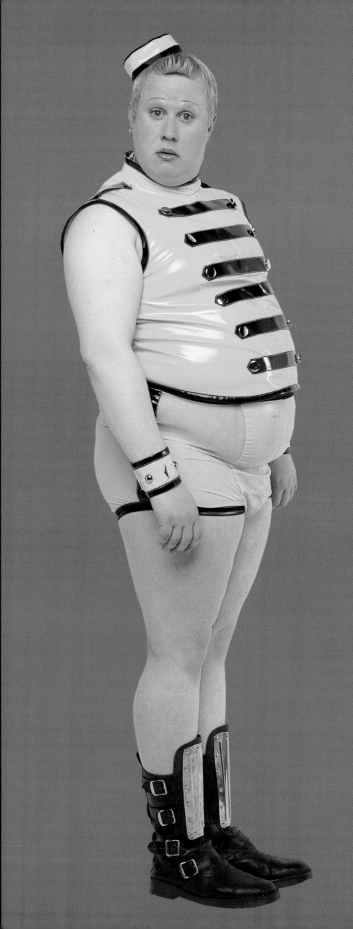

HarperCollins*Entertainment*
An Imprint of HarperCollins*Publishers*
77–85 Fulham Palace Road,
Hammersmith, London W6 8JB

www.harpercollins.co.uk

Published by HarperCollins*Entertainment* 2006

1 3 5 7 9 8 6 4 2

Text and Little Britain copyright © Matt Lucas
and David Walliams 2006

Design by Ray Barnett – BookDesign.UK.Com

A catalogue record for this book
is available from the British Library

ISBN-13   978-0-00-721365-8
ISBN-10   0-00-721365-4

Set in Rotis and Akzidenz

Printed and bound in Italy by L.E.G.O. SpA

Photographs on pages 1, 13, 23, 32-33, 34, 35, 38,
43, 54, 55 (top), 56-57, 73, 75, 96, 97, 93, 111, 114,
119, 125, 138-139, 150-151, 154-155, 157, 158-159,
176, 180, 186, 189-189, 196, 197, 198-199, 200,
201, 205, 210-211, 220 (bottom), 230-231, 232, 238
(bottom), 239, 243, 254, 255 © BBC Picture Library

Photographs on pages 3, 4, 5, 6, 7, 22, 76, 128, 166,
202 © Granada Ventures

Images on pages 46, 52, 76, 81, 82, 91, 105 (top),
116, 117, 121, 164, 167 (top), 169, 203 (bottom),
206, 208 (bottom), 209 (bottom), 215, 216 (top),
220 (top), 250, 251, 252 © BBC

All other photographs © David Walliams and
Lisa Cavalli-Green

Illustration on pages 132-3 by Bill Houston

Britain, Britain, Britain, we have exported so many great things around the world: slavery, hooliganism and Starlight Express. But none of this would have been possible without the people of Britain. Today now we look at what they, boom boom boom, let me hear you say way-oh, way-oh, bring it on!

Charged with criminal damage and gross indecency

■ by KEVIN McGEE

NEIGHBOUR WATCH leader was arrested yesterday for spying on his neighbour.

It is alleged that Sid Pegg, 58, drilled a hole from his guest bedroom into the bathroom of the house next door, where widow Rosalie Bennet, 54, regularly showered.

heavy breathing

She called the police when she heard heavy breathing and then saw the squinting eye peeping through the hole.

Pegg was arrested but told police he was merely carrying out his duties as self-elected Neighbour Watch leader for Larchwood Close.

Pegg told reporters, "I was checking that there were no asylum seekers hiding behind the Radox. Also I had concerns that the Close could become a target for international terrorist organisations. Luckily, in this case, there were none present.

large nipples

I would like to add that I was in no way spying on her for my own sexual gratification, as her nipples were a bit large for my taste."

Despite his protests, Pegg has been charged with criminal damage and gross indecency: "I will take this to the Court of European Rights. I must go now as The Equaliser is on."

The gossip, the scandal, the celebs, the truth
every day!

SIMPLY THE BEST 7 DAYS A WEEK

You asked for it! You got it! EXCLUSIVE

★ Our Star Stunnas Bubbles and Desiree got all hot and steamy in this exclusive for Star readers. Phwoar! Bubbles, 19, said, 'I've always been a big fan of Desiree's. I've always wanted to meet her.' Desiree, 21, added, 'It was the sexiest shoot I've ever done. Bubbles is one fit chick.'

acknowledgements

Matt and David would like to thank everyone who appeared in series three – Tom Baker, Rob Brydon, Anthony Head, Cat Deeley, Judy Finnigan, Nigel Havers, Richard Madeley, Derek Martin, David Baddiel, Ruth Madoc, Imelda Staunton and everyone else who appeared, including Stephen Aintree, Keith Alexander, Joanna Bacon, Sam Beazley, David Benson, Su Bhoopongsa, Jiggy Bhore, Di Botcher, Anjali Mya Chadha, Paul Charlton, Charubala Chokshi, Sheila Collings, Joann Condon, Rebecca Cooper, Naomi Cooper-Davis, Deddie Davies, Patricia England, Cheryl Fergison, David Foxxe, Richard Freeman, Steve Furst, Stirling Gallacher, Kerry Gibson, Georgie Glen, James Greene, Sally Hawkins, Mike Hayward, Akiya Henry, Margaret Hilder, Nazneen Hoseini, Margaret John, Ruth Jones, Sody Singh Kahlon, Barbara Keogh, Ranjit Krishnama, Yuki Kushida, Joshua Lawton, Phoenix Lee, Freddie Lees, Geoff Leesley, Janette Legge, Aimee Liddel, Steven Lim, Joan Linder, Alice Lowe, Jennie Lucey, Damian Lynch, Elliot Perry Mason, Diana May, Anita Mohan, Habib Nasib Nader, Gordon Peters, Gregory Pitt, Paul Putner, Kirris Riviere, Sally Rogers, Leelo Ross, Danny Sapani, Shend, Harmage Singh, Annelli Smith, Gordon Sterne, Mark Stobbart, Margaret Towner, Menna Trussler, Maryann Turner, Carrigan Van Der Merwe, Indira Varma, Eleanor Vickers, Matthew Ward and Dean Whatton.

Thanks also to everyone who worked on the show, including our stunt co-ordinator Andreas Petrides, Andie Vining (prop master) and the prop team, our vision mixer Ros Storey, Greg Shaw (art director), our dubbing mixer Rob Butler-Biggs, Sarah Hollingsworth and the production team, production co-ordinator Charlotte Lamb, script supervisor Chrissie Bibby, our editor Mykola Pawluk, production manager and cub scout choirmaster Francis Gilson, director of photography Katie Swain, the greatest production designer in the land – Dennis de Groot (no relation), production buyer Jac Hyman, our brilliant costume designer Annie Hardinge and her team (Sheena Gunn, Janine Marr, Aaron Timperly), Bronwyn at the Business, the BBC Costume Store, Angels and, of course, Chris de Witt and all at Carlo Manzi's, our wonderful make-up designer Lisa Cavalli-Green and her team (Nicola Coleman and Suzi Munachen), BBC Wigstore, Richard Mawbury and all at Wig Specialities, on cameras . . . Nigel Saunders, John Sorapure, the camera team (David Penfold, Kirk Thornton, Bart Tuft, Ross Turley), John Currie, Nick Robertson and Jem Whippey in the sound dept, Thomas Howard for finding all the locations, David Arnold (who done all the music), our script editor Richard Herring, Ted Robbins for studio warm-ups, stage manager Caroline Caley, our ever-smiling studio resource manager Andrew Garnett, 1st AD Andy Lumsden, executive producers Myfanwy Moore and Jon Plowman, Declan Lowney for directing the whole thing, and last but not least, our fantastic producer Geoff Posner. We'd also like to say thanks to our agents Connor and Melanie, Barbara, Moira and all at MBC and BBC Publicity, and to Julian Bellamy at BBC3 and Peter Fincham at BBC1 for allowing us to dress up as ladies and do silly voices on your otherwise reputable channels.

Goodfly.

foreword by meera sharma

62 Beechcroft Drive,
New Malden, Surrey SM3 4SA

11th September 2006

Dear Reader,

Enjoy book.

Meera

EPISODE one

TOM V/O: Britain, Britain, Britain, a bloody lovely place to live. Discovered in 1972, lost in 1974, then found again a few years later hiding under Belgium. But what makes Britain so fandabidozi? Why, it's the great British public. Aah, push it, push it, ah, push it, push it real good.

BUBBLES DEVERE – ROMAN

EXT: HILL GRANGE HEALTH SPA.

TOM V/O: At Hill Grange Health Spa ex-Olympic gymnast Bubbles DeVere is off to have her breakfast.

BUBBLES APPROACHES THE MAIN ENTRANCE AND PASSES A STAFF MEMBER.

BUBBLES: Morning darling. I'm just going for breakfast. Please service my room. Quickly, chop chop, hurry up, do it quickly, thank you darling.

INT: HILL GRANGE HEALTH SPA. DINING ROOM. VARIOUS PEOPLE ARE HAVING BREAKFAST. BUBBLES, IN HER ROBE, IS AT THE BUFFET.

STAFF MEMBER/FENELLA: Are you sticking to your diet, Mrs DeVere?

BUBBLES: Oh yes, Fenella. I'm just having Special K this morning.

BUBBLES TURNS CARRYING HER TRAY, WHICH HAS FIFTY VARIETY PACK-SIZED BOXES OF SPECIAL K PILED HIGH AND A SMALL BOWL. SHE WALKS PAST SOME GUESTS, WHO ARE ALL DINING.

BUBBLES: Hello girls, hello Gita darling! Don't forget I'm having a fondue facial at twelve. (CALLS LOUDLY) Hello Mrs Popodopolos, how was your anal bleaching?

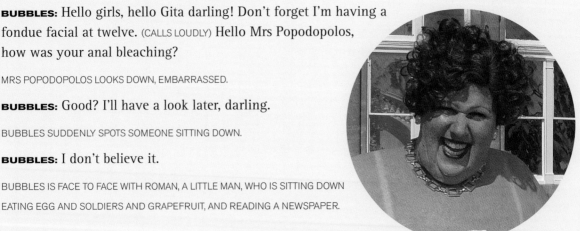

MRS POPODOPOLOS LOOKS DOWN, EMBARRASSED.

BUBBLES: Good? I'll have a look later, darling.

BUBBLES SUDDENLY SPOTS SOMEONE SITTING DOWN.

BUBBLES: I don't believe it.

BUBBLES IS FACE TO FACE WITH ROMAN, A LITTLE MAN, WHO IS SITTING DOWN EATING EGG AND SOLDIERS AND GRAPEFRUIT, AND READING A NEWSPAPER.

Hippo like you belong in the zoo.

ROMAN: Oh. Hello Bubbles. I didn't know you were staying here.

BUBBLES: I haven't seen you since the diworce.

ROMAN: Well, I thought it was better if we didn't communicate for a while.

BUBBLES: Are you here with... her?

ROMAN: If you mean Desiree, then yes.

BUBBLES: Oh goody. So I'm finally gonna meet the woman who destroyed our marri-age. Is she... as beautiful as they say?

ROMAN: I think so. Yes. (TO DESIREE) Darling?

AN ENORMOUS BLACK LADY APPEARS, CARRYING A TRAY WITH A SINGLE YOGHURT ON IT.

DESIREE: Yes?

ROMAN: Desiree, I don't believe you've met my ex-wife, Bubbles.

DESIREE: (UNIMPRESSED) Hello baby, so nice to meet you.

DESIREE AND ROMAN SIT DOWN. SHE DRAPES HERSELF OVER HIM. AS FAR AS SHE IS CONCERNED, HER CONVERSATION WITH BUBBLES IS OVER.

DESIREE: Don't forget, sugar, we have our honeymoon massage at ten.

ROMAN: Nice to see you again, Bubbles.

A DEFEATED BUBBLES GOES TO LEAVE. DESIREE BEGINS CHUCKLING. BUBBLES HALTS.

BUBBLES: I wouldn't have that Munch Bunch yoghurt if I were you, darling.

DESIREE: Why's that, baby?

BUBBLES: You already look like a hippo, darling.

DESIREE: Oh do I, baby?

BUBBLES: Yeah, baby.

BUBBLES THROWS HER TRAY ONTO A TABLE. SHE TURNS TO DESIREE.

BUBBLES: Hippo like you belong in the zoo.

DESIREE SCOWLS.

ROMAN: Desiree, please.

DESIREE RISES TO HER FEET.

DESIREE: Maybe baby's right. Maybe I shouldn't have this Munch Bunch raspberry yoghurt after all.

DESIREE OPENS HER YOGHURT AND CAREFULLY POURS THE CONTENTS OVER BUBBLES.

BUBBLES: You little slut.

DESIREE: You fat bitch!

BUBBLES DELIVERS A SLAP TO DESIREE'S FACE.

DESIREE: Get your hands off me!

DESIREE RIPS BUBBLES' ROBE OFF; BUBBLES RETURNS THE FAVOUR. BOTH NAKED, THEY FALL TO THE FLOOR, ROLLING AROUND.

GITA: Please, stop them!

ROMAN: (WATCHING WITH RESTRAINED EXCITEMENT) Let's not be too hasty.

LOU AND ANDY — AQUARIUM

TOM V/O: In the words of the famous song, 'This is the dawning of the Age of the Aquarium'.

INT: AQUARIUM. LOU IS WHEELING ANDY ALONG.

LOU: Look, Andy, a cuttlefish.

ANDY: Yeah, I know.

LOU: (READING FROM HIS GUIDE BOOK) A cuttlefish lives in more tropical climes, and feeds on plankton.

ANDY: Yeah, I know.

LOU: Are you enjoying the aquarium, Andy?

ANDY: It's boring.

LOU: (KNEELING) But I thought you loved sea life. I thought you said that the underwater world had a sublime beauty that mankind as a species could scarcely comprehend.

ANDY: Yeah I know. I thought we was going swimming though.

Are you enjoying the aquarium, 'Andy?

LOU: Oh no, this is an aquarium. You go swimming in a swimming pool.

ANDY: Yeah, I know.

LOU: Well then. Let's see if I can find the octopuses.

LOU STANDS AND APPROACHES AN EMPLOYEE. AS HE DOES SO, ANDY GETS OUT OF HIS WHEELCHAIR UNNOTICED, AND DISAPPEARS.

LOU: (TO EMPLOYEE) Excuse me, aquarium employee. Could you tell me where the octopuses are?

EMPLOYEE: We have a few octopi. They're just down the next corridor, past the seahorses.

LOU: Oh, it's octopi is it?

EMPLOYEE: Yes.

LOU: What did I say?

EMPLOYEE: Octopuses.

LOU: Oh silly me... Always getting me pusses and me pie mixed up. Have you any eels?

Oh no, this is an aquarium. You go swimming in a swimming pool.

EMPLOYEE: Certainly, we have some eels. If you just go past there, over the next corridor to the right, you'll get some electric eels.

LOU: Oh really. Any conga eels?

EMPLOYEE: I'm afraid not.

IN THE SHARK TANK BEHIND THEM WE SEE ANDY, IN TRUNKS AND GOGGLES, SWIM PAST.

DUDLEY AND TING TONG – ARRIVAL

EXT: FLATS. BALCONY.

TOM V/O: At the Mike McShane estate in Bruise, a long-awaited visitor has finally arrived.

WE SEE THE BACK OF A WOMAN HEADING TOWARDS THE FRONT DOOR OF ONE OF THE FLATS.

INT: DUDLEY'S DINGY FLAT. A SEEDY-LOOKING MAN (DUDLEY) IN HIS FIFTIES, DRESSED AS BEST AS HE CAN, POTTERS ABOUT ANXIOUSLY, TIDYING UP. HE LOOKS THROUGH A BROCHURE WHICH READS 'THAI BRIDES FOR YOU'.

DUDLEY: Not long now my sweet.

HE KISSES THE BROCHURE. THE DOORBELL RINGS. DUDLEY SPRAYS AIR FRESHENER EVERYWHERE, INCLUDING HIS ARMPITS, AND CHECKS HIS APPEARANCE IN THE MIRROR. HE ANSWERS THE DOOR. ON THE DOORSTEP STANDS TING TONG, A SMALL, FAT SMILING THAI GIRL, HOLDING SOME FLOWERS AND A SMALL SUITCASE.

DUDLEY: No!

TING TONG: Hello Mr. Dudwey.

DUDLEY: No. No. (SHAKING HIS HEAD) You're not Ting Tong.

Not long now my sweet.

TING TONG: I am Ting Tong. Ting Tong Macadangdang.

DUDLEY: Wait there!

DUDLEY GOES INTO HIS POKEY LIVING ROOM AND PICKS UP THE BROCHURE. HE FLICKS THROUGH THE
PAGES TO FIND ONE THAT HAS A PICTURE OF AN ATTRACTIVE THIN YOUNG THAI WOMAN ON IT, WITH THE NAME
'TING TONG' UNDERNEATH.

TING TONG: Oh so this home now.

TING TONG HAS FOLLOWED HIM IN.

DUDLEY: No! I said 'wait at the door'. Look –

HE HOLDS UP THE PICTURE TO TING TONG'S FACE.

DUDLEY: – you're not 'Ting Tong'.

TING TONG: No, I am Ting Tong. That is me. Yeah, is good
photo. I give you that. Is good photo.

DUDLEY: I want my deposit back.

TING TONG: Come sit with Ting Tong.

THEY SIT

TING TONG: Let us know each other before we have good time. (REHEARSED) So, I am Ting
Tong. I am from village tiny in Thailand. I am nineteen. I am beautician. Here is picture
of my family. Hopefully they come live with us soon.

TING TONG FLICKS OPEN A LONG PHOTO WALLET THAT UNRAVELS DOWNWARDS AND DISPLAYS DOZENS OF PHOTOS
OF DIFFERENT THAI RELATIVES.

DUDLEY: I'm sorry. You're gonna have to leave.

DUDLEY USHERS TING TONG TO THE DOOR.

TING TONG: But I want be good wife
of you.

TING TONG LOOKS SAD. DUDLEY WARMS A LITTLE.

DUDLEY: Look, I'm sure you're a very pleasant
lady and I know you've had a long journey –

TING TONG: Much of it on foot.

DUDLEY: – much of it on foot, but I paid
eighty pounds. I think somebody's sold me
up the swannee.

No, I am Ting Tong. That is me. Yeah, is good photo. I give you that. Is good photo.

TING TONG: But I am love you.

DUDLEY: Well I'm very flattered but you're gonna have to leave.

TING TONG STARTS TO CRY.

TING TONG: You think I am ugwy, don't you?

DUDLEY: No... no one's saying you're hideous. Oh, there's obviously been some kind of administrational error. Look, you nip back to Thailand and we'll sort it all out from there.

TING TONG: Please don't make me leave, Mr Dudley. Please.

DUDLEY: No! I said no.

TING TONG: Mr Dudley!

DUDLEY: No. Now come on.

TING TONG: Please don't make me leave. Please, Mr. Dudley, please!

TING TONG GETS DOWN ON HER KNEES. TEARFULLY SHE HUGS HIM, HER HEAD JUST BELOW HIS WAIST, INNOCENTLY WIPING HER TEARY FACE ON HIS TROUSERS. DUDLEY LOOKS CONFLICTED.

DUDLEY: Maybe just stay tonight and we'll... see what happens.

DUDLEY STROKES HER ON THE HEAD.

Maybe just stay tonight and we'll... see what happens.

VICKY POLLARD — DANCE OFF

EXT: DAY. RECREATION AREA OF A COUNCIL ESTATE.

TOM V/O: After a productive morning sending bullying text messages to younger children, Vicky and her gang are returning to their estate.

VICKY AND HER GANG ARE ON THE PROWL. THEY TURN A CORNER AND SPOT A GROUP OF SIMILARLY-ATTIRED TEENAGE GIRLS PRACTISING DANCE MOVES. THEY HAVE A GHETTO BLASTER PLAYING COOL HIP-HOP. VICKY IS SMOKING.

VICKY: Who the Hollyoaks Omnibus is that?

KELLY: That's Chantelle Bacon's gang.

VICKY: Who or summin' or nuffin'?

ROCHELLE: They live down St Pauls.

VICKY: No but yeah but no but what are they doin' on our patch or summin' or nuffin' or sorta, like, fing, because (RAISING VOLUME) they are well gonna get beatings.

KELLY: Cool it, Vicky. They are well hard.

MELODY: Yeah, they gave the Redmond sisters a bogwash.

VICKY: They don't scare me. Don't be fooled by the rocks that I got. I'm just Vicky Pollard from round the corner from the block.

VICKY STRIKES A POSE TOWARDS THE RIVAL GANG.

VICKY: V to the P to the Icky to the Ollard. Oh my god. This is well hectic.

VICKY APPROACHES THE RIVAL GANG. ONE BY ONE THEY NOTICE VICKY AND HER MOB AND STOP AND STAND, PROVOCATIVELY, FORMING A GROUP.

VICKY: Hey you. What you doing on our patch, you total bunch of mingin' dog bitches?

ONE TOUGH-LOOKING GIRL MAKES HER WAY TO THE FRONT OF THE GROUP. IT LOOKS LIKE A FIGHT MIGHT BE ABOUT TO START BUT INSTEAD, THE MUSIC STEPS UP A GEAR AND THE RIVAL LEADER DOES AN IMPRESSIVE DANCE MOVE, SNAPPING HER FINGERS AS SHE FINISHES. HER GANG LOOK SMUG.

IN RESPONSE, VICKY DOES A RUBBISH BODYPOPPING/ROBOTICS DANCE, TOPPED OFF WITH A NAFF MIME. HER MOB TRY TO BE SUPPORTIVE, WHILE CRINGING.

A SECOND GIRL FROM THE RIVAL GANG DOES A WILDLY PHYSICAL MOVE, BREAKDANCING ON THE FLOOR, SPINNING ROUND. VICKY GETS DOWN ON HER BACK AND SIGNALS TO HER FRIENDS. SHE REMAINS STILL AND HER FRIENDS SPIN HER ROUND. SHE SITS UP IN AN UNGAINLY WAY AND STRIKES A TRIUMPHANT POSE.

THE RIVAL GANG DO A CO-ORDINATED DANCE MOVE THEN A THIRD GANG MEMBER STEPS FORWARD, DOES A BACKFLIP AND THEN SIGNS OFF TRIUMPHANTLY IN VICKY'S FACE.

VICKY TAKES A DRAG ON HER CIGARETTE THEN HANDS IT TO ONE OF HER MOB. SHE SAUNTERS FORWARD THEN TWEAKS THE GIRL'S NIPPLE. THE GIRL RECOILS. THE RIVAL GANG RETREATS. VICKY AND GANG DO A VICTORY STRUT OFF.

VICKY: We is well the best dancers.

MRS EMERY — SUPERMARKET

TOM V/O: Mrs Emery is what we, in Britain, call an OAP, which stands for Old And Putrid.

INT: SUPERMARKET. MRS EMERY, A VERY CHIRPY OUTGOING OLD LADY, WITH A SHOPPING BASKET, IS TICKING ITEMS OFF HER SHOPPING LIST.

MRS EMERY: Right. Apple. Need an apple.

A SLIGHTLY YOUNGER LADY, JUNE, STOPS HER.

JUNE: Hello Mrs Emery.

MRS EMERY: Oh hallo, dear.

JUNE: I met you at the jumble sale the other day.

Oh hallo, dear.

MRS EMERY: Oh yeah.

JUNE: I hear they raised a lot of money.

MRS EMERY: Oh that's good, 'cause they need that new roof.

AT THIS MOMENT, WITHOUT BATTING AN EYELID, MRS EMERY STARTS PEEING HEAVILY ON THE FLOOR, AS IF SOMEBODY WAS POURING A BUCKET OUT FROM BETWEEN HER LEGS. SHE MAINTAINS EYE CONTACT, WHILST JUNE LOOKS PERTURBED.

MRS EMERY: Did you meet the new vicar that day?

JUNE: (STARING DOWN) Y-yes. Yes.

MRS EMERY: Very nice, isn't he? Young for a vicar but very very nice. Lovely smile.

JUNE STARTS TO BACK OFF, AS MRS EMERY'S SEEMINGLY ENDLESS PEE CONTINUES TO FLOW.

JUNE: Yes, he was nice.

MRS EMERY: Did you pick up anything at the sale?

JUNE: No. Not really.

MRS. EMERY MOVES FORWARDS AND GRABS JUNE'S HAND.

MRS EMERY: I got a lovely book on handicrafts and a very nice set of thimbles.

JUNE: Oh... lovely.

MRS EMERY: Well, I can't stand here chatting all day. I'll see you later, dear.

MRS EMERY GOES TO LEAVE.

MRS EMERY: Oh mind out. Someone's spilt something. Ta ta.

MRS EMERY WANDERS OFF, LEAVING A SHOCKED JUNE STARING DOWN AT THE VAST POOL OF URINE.

I, um, think you may have forgotten something, my dear.

EMILY AND FLORENCE — BEARD

EXT: SEASIDE/PARADE OF SHOPS.

TOM V/O: In Britain, we can proudly say we have transvestites from all walks of life. Between 1979 and 1990 even the British Prime Minister was a transvestite.

FLORENCE IS STANDING BY A PLASTIC 99 ICE CREAM CONE AND CHECKING HER WATCH, WAITING FOR EMILY ON THE SEAFRONT. EMILY APPROACHES BRISKLY, BLISSFULLY UNAWARE THAT SHE HAS A VERY FULL, QUITE LONG BEARD.

EMILY: Sorry I'm late, Florence. I overslept.

FLORENCE: I, um, think you may have forgotten something, my dear.

EMILY: Oh really, what's that?

FLORENCE: Er, well, er, ah, come with me, my dear.

FLORENCE TAKES EMILY BY THE HAND AND LEADS HER TOWARDS A NEARBY VENDING MACHINE. SHE SHOWS EMILY HER REFLECTION.

EMILY: Oh, this is exciting.

FLORENCE: Regardez...

EMILY: Oh, do my earrings not go with my – (REALISING) Ooooh! Florence, help me! I'm a lady with a beard! Help me!

FLORENCE: Calm down, dear!

EMILY: I can't calm down! I'm a bearded lady!

FLORENCE: What happened?

EMILY: I forgot to shave this morning. It grows so fast, doesn't it?

Oh, do my earrings not go with my — Ooooh! Florence, help me! I'm a lady with a beard! Help me!

FLORENCE: Here, take this.

FLORENCE HANDS HER A JAPANESE FAN. EMILY TAKES IT AND USES IT TO CONCEAL HER FACE.

EMILY: What am I to do?

FLORENCE: I don't know. Um. There's a chemist over there. They may have something for you.

INT: CHEMIST. A LADY IS SERVING BEHIND THE COUNTER. EMILY AND FLORENCE ENTER. EMILY IS STILL CONCEALING HER FULL BEARD WITH THE FAN.

LADY: Yes, gents?

FLORENCE: My *ladyfriend* here needs to talk to you about something rather embarrassing.

EMILY: Yes. I have a very slight facial hair problem.

LADY: Can I see?

EMILY REMOVES THE FAN. THE LADY LOOKS SUITABLY HORRIFIED.

EMILY: It's not very noticeable, I know, but I know it's there and it's not very ladylike, is it?

EPISODE

LADY: No. Well, the razors are over there.

EMILY: I can't use a razor. I am a lady.

LADY: Well, some ladies who come here with your... problem...

EMILY: Problem? Yes.

LADY: ...they like to use this. It bleaches the hair.

SHE SHOWS EMILY THE BLEACH.

EMILY: I see. And this is for ladies, is it?

LADY: Yes.

EMILY: Very well. I'll take twelve tubs.

LADY: (TO FLORENCE) Would you like to take a tub?

FLORENCE: I beg your pardon?

LADY: Well, you do have a slight moustache problem.

EMILY NODS SUBTLY IN AGREEMENT TO THE LADY.

FLORENCE: (INDIGNANT) How dare you?!

EMILY: (DEEP VOICE) You do. (MOUTHS TO THE LADY) He does!

EXT: CHEMIST DOORWAY. EMILY AND FLORENCE ARE EXITING. EMILY HAS THE FAN IN FRONT OF HER MOUTH AGAIN. EMILY PAUSES.

EMILY: Are you sure you can't see it?

FLORENCE: Honestly, my dear, you wouldn't know it was there.

EMILY LETS DOWN THE FAN TO REVEAL THAT THE BEARD IS NOW WHITE (BUT STILL VERY NOTICEABLE). EMILY AND FLORENCE LINK ARMS, SMILING, THEN WALK ALONG THE SEAFRONT

SIR NORMAN FRY – RASTAFARIAN

EXT: COUNTRY ESTATE.

TOM V/O: In Buxom, Sir Norman Fry, MP, has called a press conference.

SIR NORMAN FRY, ARMS LINKED HIS WIFE CAMILLA AND THEIR YOUNG SON AND DAUGHTER, APPROACHES THE GATE AT THE END OF THE DRIVE. WAITING FOR THEM IS A LARGE GROUP OF JOURNALISTS, PHOTOGRAPHERS AND TV CREWS. SIR NORMAN, IN A CASHMERE PULLOVER, HAS HIS ARM ROUND CAMILLA, WHO IS PUTTING ON A BRAVE FACE. THE CHILDREN LOOK EMBARRASSED. SIR NORMAN TAKES OUT A PIECE OF PAPER.

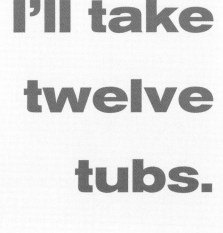

Very well. I'll take twelve tubs.

At this point I fell on top of him and I regret to say a part of my body accidentally entered him. As far as I am concerned that is the end of the matter. Thank you.

PRESS: Sir Norman! Sir Norman! When are you resigning? etc.

SIR NORMAN: I have a statement I'd like to read. On Tuesday night, following a late meeting at party headquarters, I decided to go for a relaxing drive through the King's Cross area. Whilst there, I saw a young Rastafarian gentleman on the side of the road. As one of my constituents, I felt it my duty to stop and offer him a lift. During the journey I pulled over into a nearby alleyway so that I could safely reach into the glove compartment and take out a Murray Mint. At this point I fell on top of him and I regret to say a part of my body accidentally entered him. As far as I am concerned that is the end of the matter. Thank you.

SIR NORMAN AWKWARDLY KISSES HIS WIFE ON THE LIPS FOR THE CAMERAS. JOURNALISTS CLAMOUR TO ASK MORE QUESTIONS.

CAROL – TORONTO

EXT: 'SUNSEARCHERS' TRAVEL AGENTS. WE SEE CAROL BEER INSIDE THE SHOP, STANDING AT THE WINDOW. SHE PINS UP A POSTER THAT READS 'KABUL – FLY-DRIVE – £99'.

TOM V/O: Carol Beer has left her job at the bank and is now delighting customers at this travel agents in the new town of SpongeBob Squarepants.

INT: TRAVEL AGENTS. CAROL BEER IS SAT AT HER DESK. AN ELDERLY MAN (MR RYAN) IS SAT IN FRONT OF HER.

CAROL: That's all booked for you, Mr Ryan – one fly-drive return to Toronto.

MR RYAN: Thank you. I'm so looking forward to it. I haven't seen my daughter in four years.

CAROL: No.

MR RYAN GETS UP TO LEAVE. HE SITS BACK DOWN AGAIN.

MR RYAN: Oh, one thing I forgot to say. Is it possible for me to have a vegetarian meal on the plane?

CAROL: I'll just have to cancel your booking...

CAROL TYPES.

MR RYAN: Oh don't do that.

CAROL: Right. Done that. So you want to fly to Toronto on the 14th?

MR RYAN: Yes.

CAROL TYPES.

CAROL: Computer says no.

MR RYAN: What?

CAROL: You had the last ticket and someone must have taken it.

MR RYAN: I just need a flight to Toronto but with a vegetarian meal.

Oh, I've got a nut rissole on a flight to Beijing. That leaves in ten minutes.

CAROL: I can get you a vegetarian meal... on a flight to Berlin. It would be leaving tonight.

MR RYAN: Look, the meal isn't that important.

CAROL: It's a lentil bake with a rocket salad.

MR RYAN: No. I don't want that.

CAROL: I'll just put that on hold for you in case you change your mind. Oh, I've got a nut rissole on a flight to Beijing. That leaves in ten minutes.

MR RYAN: No.

CAROL STARES AT THE SCREEN.

CAROL: I've got a piece of marinated tofu on a flight to Vancouver.

MR RYAN: Vancouver... that could work.

I've got a piece of marinated tofu on a flight to Vancouver.

CAROL: It's taxiing now. If you run you might just get it.

MR RYAN: Obviously not, then.

CAROL: No.

MR RYAN: Can I get to Toronto the following day instead?

CAROL: Computer says no.

MR RYAN: You didn't even type anything in, then.

CAROL HITS A KEY WITHOUT LOOKING.

CAROL: Computer says no.

MR RYAN: (SARACASTICALLY) Thank you very much.

CAROL: Oh, hang on. Hang on.

MR RYAN RETURNS TO THE DESK.

MR RYAN: Yes?

CAROL COUGHS IN HIS FACE.

CAROL: (SMILING) Goodbye.

DAFYDD – RENTBOY

TOM V/O: Over in the Welsh mining village of Llandewi Breffi, little fat poofer Dafydd Thomas has finally found a vocation in life.

EXT: VILLAGE. DAFYDD MARCHES DOWN THE STREET, WEARING A VERY SKIMPY, LATEX AND PVC OUTFIT. HE PASSES A FRIENDLY-LOOKING LOLLIPOP LADY.

LOLLIPOP LADY: Evening Dafydd.

DAFYDD: Yeah, I'm gay. Get with the programme!

INT: PUB. A VERY OLD MAN IN A FLAT CAP (MR JENKINS) IS SAT AT THE BAR.

If it gets you some bumfun I'm all for it.

MYFANWY: There's your port, Mr Jenkins.

MR JENKINS: Thank you, love.

DAFYDD ENTERS AND SLOWLY WALKS TO THE BAR, FLAUNTING HIS BODY.

MYFANWY: Evening Dafydd.

DAFYDD: Good evening, Myfanwy. I think I'll have a Bacardi and Coke, please.

MYFANWY: Coming right up. That's a very skimpy little number you're wearing there.

DAFYDD: Mmm, it's for my new job.

MYFANWY: Oh yes?

DAFYDD: Yes. I have become a rent boy.

MYFANWY: A rent boy.

DAFYDD: That's right, Myfanwy. I've got the looks, I've got the body. I'm a young gay guy. Why shouldn't I just go for it?

MYFANWY: How's business?

DAFYDD: Slow... but tonight is the first night.

MYFANWY: And have you advertised?

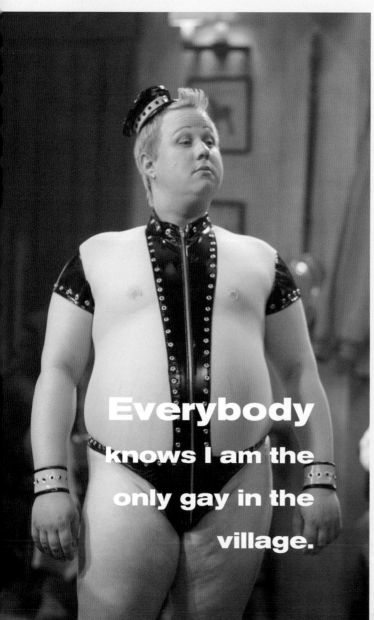

Everybody knows I am the only gay in the village.

DAFYDD: Yes, Mrs Jones has put a card up in the post office and the vicar has very kindly said he'll give me a mention in the parish news.

MYFANWY: Well, Dafydd. If it gets you some bumfun I'm all for it.

DAFYDD: Well, I very much doubt I'll pick up any trade, Myfanwy. Everybody knows I am the only gay in the village.

DAFYDD TAKES A DRINK. A BURLY MIDDLE-AGED BEARDED MAN IN A MINER'S OUTFIT (BRIAN) ENTERS THE PUB.

BRIAN: Excuse me, are you Scott?

DAFYDD LOOKS BRIEFLY TAKEN ABACK.

DAFYDD: Oh, um, yes.

MYFANWY: I'll leave you boys to it.

MYFANWY GOES TO THE OTHER END OF THE BAR AND SERVES A CUSTOMER.

DAFYDD: (UNCOMFORTABLE) No don't go, I...

BRIAN: It said in the advert you looked like Dermot O'Leary.

It said in the advert you looked like Dermot O'Leary.

That's right, yes. In his younger days.

DAFYDD: That's right, yes. In his younger days.

BRIAN: Well, you're not quite what I expected but I've had an hard day so have you got somewhere we can go?

DAFYDD: Yes, well I thought we'd go to Mrs. Evans' tearooms and have a scone, and then I thought we could have a wander round some of the charity shops –

BRIAN: That's not quite what I had in mind, Scott.

DAFYDD: Who's Scott?

BRIAN: You are.

DAFYDD: Oh yes.

BRIAN: How much for a good hard shag?

DAFYDD: (PANICKING) Myfanwy!

MYFANWY: I'm serving Mr Jenkins.

DAFYDD: Look, I only hold hands on a first date.

BRIAN: Bloody timewaster!

BRIAN EXITS. MYFANWY RETURNS.

DAFYDD: I think you better give me another Bacardi and Coke please, Myfanwy!

MYFANWY: Dafydd Thomas, what are you like? Rent boy indeed.

DAFYDD: Yes, I better go and see Mrs Jones and ask her to take that advert down.

MYFANWY: Yes, first thing tomorrow.

MYFANWY GOES OFF TO SERVE SOMEONE ELSE. MEANWHILE A VERY BIG, TALL, HAIRY FIFTY-YEAR-OLD WITH A LARGE MOUSTACHE AND IN LEATHERS APPEARS OVER DAFYDD'S SHOULDER.

LEATHER MAN: Scott?

DAFYDD SIGNALS TOWARDS MR JENKINS, WHO, BLISSFULLY UNAWARE, IS STILL SIPPING HIS PORT.

DAFYDD: Just over there.

LEATHER MAN: Thank you.

THE LEATHER MAN HEADS TOWARDS MR JENKINS. DAFYDD TIPTOES OUT, GUILTILY.

How much for a good hard shag?

ANNE – STARS IN THEIR EYES

TOM V/O: In Gash, Dr Lawrence is showing Dr Beagrie how one of his patients is progressing.

INT: DR LAWRENCE'S STUDY. DR LAWRENCE SITS WITH DR BEAGRIE. DR LAWRENCE LOOKS AT HIS WATCH.

DR. LAWRENCE: Oh, goodness. It's nearly time.

HE GETS UP AND USES THE REMOTE TO SWITCH ON THE TELEVISION.

DR LAWRENCE: This is going to prove just how far Anne has come in the last six months. It'll be wonderful for her self-confidence. It'll also tell everybody a lot about the hospital too!

DR LAWRENCE TURNS ON THE TV.

INT: *STARS IN THEIR EYES* STUDIO. ON TELLY, CAT DEELEY IS STANDING ON THE *STARS IN THEIR EYES* SET. SHE INTRODUCES THE NEXT CONTESTANT.

CAT: But now, it's been her dream to be on the show for many years. Ladies and gentleman, please welcome, Anne!

ON TELLY, ANNE WALKS ON STAGE, ACKNOWLEDGING THE AUDIENCE AS SHE APPROACHES CAT. SHE STANDS FACING CAT DEELEY.

CAT: Hi Anne, thanks for coming on the show. Lovely cardigan.

ANNE: Thank you.

CAT: Now, tell me, do you have any funny stories that have happened to you over the years.

ANNE: No.

CAT: Okay, er, so tell me a little bit about the person you're going to be. Give us your clues.

Eh eheh eh ehh eh, eh ehh ehh...

ANNE: She's originally from Quebec, she represented Switzerland in the Eurovision Song Contest, she sung the theme tune to *Titanic*, and she's got an old, fat husband with a beard.

CAT: (SLIGHTLY THROWN) Okay, er, so tell us Anne, who are you going to be tonight?

ANNE: Tonight, Matthew, I'm going to be Celine Dion.

CAT: Celine Dion! (KISSING ANNE) Good luck, enjoy it, off you go!

IN THE STUDY, DR LAWRENCE BEAMS AT DR. BEAGRIE.

CAT: She helps out every other Wednesday at a charity shop in Hawley, but tonight, singing live, Anne is... Celine Dion!

TO AUDIENCE APPLAUSE, ANNE WAVES AND WALKS THROUGH THE SLIDING DOOR. A MOMENT LATER, SHE EMERGES IN A BEAUTIFUL DRESS AS CELINE DION. THE ORCHESTRA PICKS OUT THE MELODY TO *MY HEART WILL GO ON* FROM *TITANIC*. THE SONG BEGINS, AND ANNE STARTS TO SING...

ANNE: Eh eheh eh ehh eh, eh ehh ehh...

THE AUDIENCE APPLAUD AS THEY RECOGNISE THE SONG. THEN ANNE LOSES INTEREST AND DROPS THE THE MICROPHONE AND KNOCKS OVER A PIECE OF SET. THE BALLAD MUSIC CONTINUES UNDERNEATH.

ANNE: Eh eh eh.

ANNE LOPES OVER TO THE CAMERA.

ANNE: Eh eh eh.

ANNE LICKS THE LENS, GRUNTING, THEN WIPES IT WITH HER HAND.

ANNE: Eh eh eh.

DR LAWRENCE: She sounds quite a lot like her, doesn't she?

LINDA — BALDY

INT: LINDA'S OFFICE. LINDA SITS OPPOSITE A YOUNG, COMPLETELY BALD GUY (ROBIN).

TOM V/O: Formerly Dudley Polytechnic, this university was opened by Sir Darren Day in 1994.

ROBIN: …yeah, but I was just wondering if I could do my extended essay on 'Modes of Sexual Discourse in the works of Jane Austen' because I know we did study that last term.

LINDA: I don't know what the rules are on this. Martin'll know.

I don't know what the rules are on this. Martin'll know.

That's better.

ROBIN: Oh, it's alright. I can go to his office.

LINDA: No, no. It's better if I phone him.

LINDA PICKS UP THE PHONE AND DIALS.

LINDA: Martin, it's Linda. I've got Robin Dashwood in front of me – wants to know if he can write his extended essay on Jane Austen.

LINDA: Robin. You know Robin. Lots of jazzy waistcoats. Colourful glasses. Always smiling. Puts you in mind of a young Elmer Fudd. Fell out of the same tree as Duncan Goodhew. Could be mistaken for a boiled egg. That's right. (SHOUTS) Baldy!

LINDA PUTS THE PHONE DOWN AND TURNS TO ROBIN.

LINDA: He says that's fine.

ROBIN: (UNIMPRESSED) Thanks very much.

ROBIN GETS UP TO LEAVE.

LINDA: Oh, could you come here for a second, Robin?

ROBIN DOES SO. LINDA PATS HIS HEAD REPEATEDLY.

LINDA: That's better.

LINDA GIVES HIS HEAD A FINAL PAT.

Could be mistaken for a boiled egg. That's right. BALDY!

EPISODE

MARJORIE DAWES/FATFIGHTERS — SPRAY TAN

INT: FATFIGHTERS. THE GROUP ARE ASSEMBLED. MARJORIE ENTERS. HER FACE AND HANDS ARE BRIGHT ORANGE.

TOM V/O: These people are what we, in Britain, fondly call fat pigs. In Sessex, Marjorie Dawes is hosting her weekly FatFighters group meeting.

MARJORIE: Hello FatFighters. Hope you've had a good week. Now today we're going to be talking about binge-eating, yes I know the spray tan went wrong. (GROUP LOOK AT EACH OTHER) So what kind of foods are binge foods? Foods that we binge on when we want to have a binge.

PAUL PUTS HIS HAND UP.

MARJORIE: Yes, Paul?

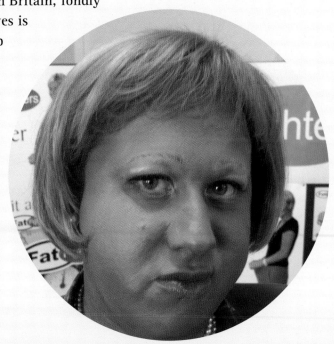

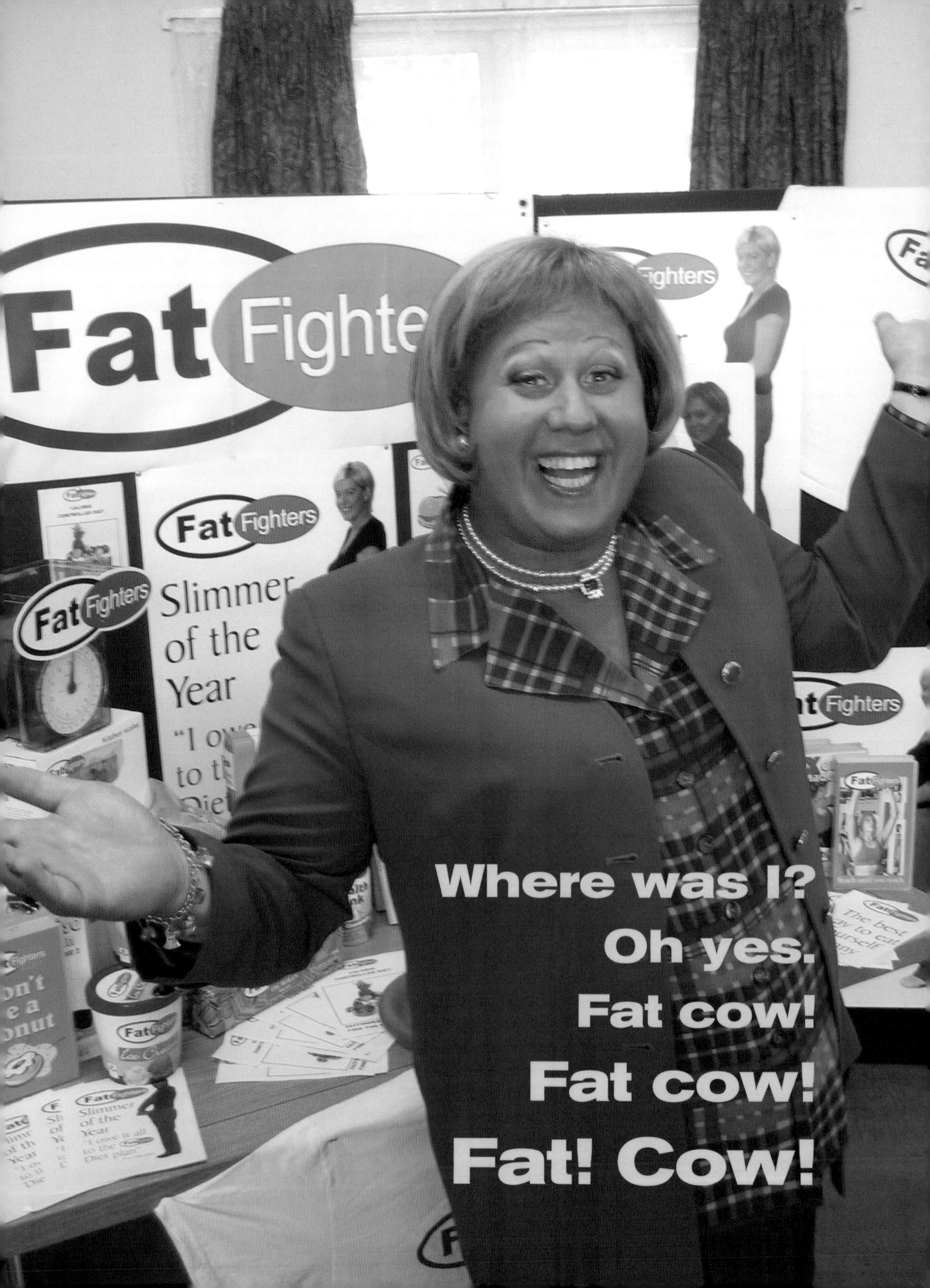

Where was I?
Oh yes.
Fat cow!
Fat cow!
Fat! Cow!

PAUL: Um, Terry's Chocolate Orange.

THE GROUP CHUCKLE.

PAUL: It comes in a big orange wrapper and it's got chocolate, and you tap it –

MARJORIE: Yes, I know what it is. Right, (WRITES ON THE BOARD) Chucklet.

MARJORIE: I did ask for St. Tropez (LOOKS AT HER HAND) but they gave me Hawaiian Sunset. Anyone else?

TANYA: For me it's fizzy drinks.

PAUL: What? Like Tango?

THERE IS MUCH LAUGHTER IN THE ROOM. MARJORIE IGNORES THIS AND WRITES ON THE BOARD.

MARJORIE: Fizzy drinks. Any more?

MEERA: Marmalade.

EVERYONE CHUCKLES.

MARJORIE: Sorry, I couldn't understand a word.

TANYA: She said marmalade.

EVERYONE LAUGHS AGAIN.

MARJORIE: Did she?

I did ask for St. Tropez but they gave me Hawaiian Sunset. Anyone else?

Sorry, I couldn't understand a word.

MARJORIE WRITES ON THE BOARD.

MARJORIE: Conserves. Any more? Any more *serious* suggestions?

PAT: Satsumas.

EVERYBODY LAUGHS AGAIN.

MARJORIE: A satsuma isn't really a binge food.

PAT: No, but it is orange.

THE GROUP ARE IN HYSTERICS.

MARJORIE: Have you quite finished?

THE LAUGHTER DIES DOWN. MARJORIE LOOKS ANGRY.

Oh man you fat.

You a big fat lady.

You fatty, fatty, fatty.

MARJORIE: I'm shocked really that you, of all people, would pick on someone for the way they look. I mean I may be orange but (RAISING VOICE) you are something else. You is fat! (IN A DEEP SOUTH ACCENT) Oh man you fat. You a big fat lady. You fatty, fatty, fatty.

THE GROUP ARE SHOCKED. MARJORIE SPOTS A LARGE LADY LOITERING BY THE DOOR.

MARJORIE: Ooh, noo member? Come and take a seat, my love. I won't be one moment. Where was I? Oh yes. (TO PAT, AS COCKNEY BLOKE) Fat cow! Fat cow! Fat! Cow!

SEBASTIAN AND MICHAEL – ARMS TO IRAN

EXT: NO. 10 DOWNING STREET. MICHAEL IS ARRIVING IN HIS CAR. THE PRESS ARE CLAMOURING TO ASK HIM QUESTIONS.

PRESS: Prime Minister. Prime Minister.

TOM V/O: If you collect enough tokens on the back of special packets of Coco Pops, you too can send off and become Prime Minister.

SEBASTIAN GREETS MICHAEL AT THE FRONT DOOR WITH A PECK ON THE CHEEK, BUT SLAMS THE DOOR WHEN GREGORY TRIES TO FOLLOW THEM IN.

INT. PM'S OFFICE. MICHAEL IS SAT AT HIS DESK, BEHIND HIM IS SEBASTIAN. OPPOSITE THE PM IS THE DOUR SCOTTISH CHANCELLOR.

CHANCELLOR: ...I hardly need to tell you, Prime Minister, it would be extremely damaging if this government were to be found selling arms to Iran.

Little
BRITAIN 🇬🇧 **45**

EPISODE

MICHAEL: Robert, let me assure you that's not what I was doing.

CHANCELLOR: Then where did *The Sunday Times* get this story from?

SEBASTIAN: Excuse me, Prime Minister. (TO CHANCELLOR) Look, dear. He said he didn't do it so he didn't do it. Honestly!

CHANCELLOR: You don't want a backbench rebellion on this, Prime Minister. There's already talk of a leadership challenge.

SEBASTIAN: Such a stirrer.

MICHAEL: Sebastian, thank you. (TO CHANCELLOR) Robert, you have my word on this.

CHANCELLOR: Very well. I shall see you at *Prime Minister's Questions*.

MICHAEL: Sebastian, would you show the Chancellor out, please?

SEBASTIAN MINCES OVER TO THE DOOR AND SHOWS THE CHANCELLOR OUT.

SEBASTIAN: (SOTTO) Just 'cause *you* wanna be Prime Minister.

CHANCELLOR: (OUTRAGED) I do not!

SEBASTIAN: You do. (TO MICHAEL) She does.

SEBASTIAN SHUTS THE DOOR.

MICHAEL: Sebastian, would you lock the door?

SEBASTIAN DOES SO.

MICHAEL: Come over here please.

SEBASTIAN QUICKLY APPROACHES MICHAEL UNTIL HE IS RIGHT IN HIS FACE.

MICHAEL: I have something rather private that I need to show you.

SEBASTIAN: (QUIETLY) Yes?

MICHAEL: Something quite sensitive.

SEBASTIAN: (HUSKILY) Um?

MICHAEL: It could be potentially very explosive.

SEBASTIAN: (LOW VOICE, AROUSED) Oh Prime Minister, I want it so bad.

MICHAEL: (FIRMLY) It's this file.

SEBASTIAN: (SNAPPING OUT OF IT) Oh yes, this file. Yes, I want this file so bad. Oh yes. What is it?

MICHAEL: It's an intelligence file that I need you to destroy for me.

SEBASTIAN: Oh. Okay.

SEBASTIAN TAKES THE FILE FROM MICHAEL AND LOOKS AT IT.

SEBASTIAN: (READS) 'Arms Deals with Iran'. (ALARMED) But you just told the Chancellor there were no arms deals with Iran.

I have something rather private that I need to show you.

MICHAEL: Yes.

SEBASTIAN: You lied. (QUIET, HURT) But I thought you were perfect.

MICHAEL: I need you to shred this.

SEBASTIAN: But if this got out it would...

A SHOCKED SEBASTIAN LOOKS AT MICHAEL. MICHAEL INDICATES TOWARDS THE DOOR.

MICHAEL: Sebastian, please. Just do this favour for me.

Don't forget the bottom shelf, Prime Minister.

SEBASTIAN: Of course, Prime Minister.

SEBASTIAN TAKES THE FILE AND HEADS FOR THE DOOR, DEEP IN THOUGHT. HE REACHES THE DOOR AND TURNS TO THE PRIME MINISTER.

SEBASTIAN: ...but first, Prime Minister, how about you do a favour for me?

MICHAEL LOOKS PUZZLED.

CUT TO: INT. OFFICE. A RELUCTANT MICHAEL, NAKED BUT FOR A POSING POUCH, IS CLEANING THE DESK WITH A FEATHER DUSTER. SEBASTIAN IS SAT ON THE SOFA WITH A CUP OF TEA.

SEBASTIAN: Don't forget the bottom shelf, Prime Minister.

MICHAEL SIGHS AND BENDS DOWN TO GET TO THE BOTTOM SHELF, GIVING SEBASTIAN A CLEAR VIEW OF HIS REAR. SEBASTIAN SMILES AND TAKES A SIP OF TEA.

LOU AND ANDY — AIRSHOW

TOM V/O: Airshows in Britain have been taking place since medieval times, although they only really became popular with the invention of the aeroplane.

EXT: AIRSHOW. CROWDS MILLING AROUND. LOU BUYS TWO ICE CREAMS FROM A VAN. HE IS SHOCKED TO RETURN TO AN EMPTY WHEELCHAIR.

LOU: Andy? Andy, where are you? Andy? Andy?!

LOU STOPS A PASSING ST JOHN AMBULANCE LADY (JEAN).

LOU: Excuse me, St. Johns Ambulance lady. Sorry to bother you. I'm looking for my friend Andy Pipkin. That's his wheelchair. I can't think what's happened to him.

JEAN: Well, I can get them to put out a call on the tannoy.

LOU: Well, I don't want to cause a whole kerfuffle.

JEAN: It's no trouble.

LOU: Well, if you wouldn't mind. I'm a bit worried and I don't want him to miss the Red Arrows.

JEAN: You wait here, and I'll get them to put out a call.

LOU: Oh, thank you very much.

JEAN EXITS. IN THE BACKGROUND ANDY PARACHUTES DOWN, LANDING SAFELY IN HIS CHAIR.

LOU: Oh Andy, where are you?

ANDY: I'm right here.

LOU: Oh, *there* you are. I was worried sick.

LOU GIVES ANDY BOTH ICE CREAMS AND STARTS TO WHEEL HIM OFF.

LOU: Is that your parachute, or...?

TOM V/O: So we say, "Farewell Little Britain". I myself must bounce now, as I did promise my homies that we would chill for a bit, have a glass or two of pimp juice and, God willing, get ourselves some sweet bootie. Bye bye!

Is that your parachute, or...?

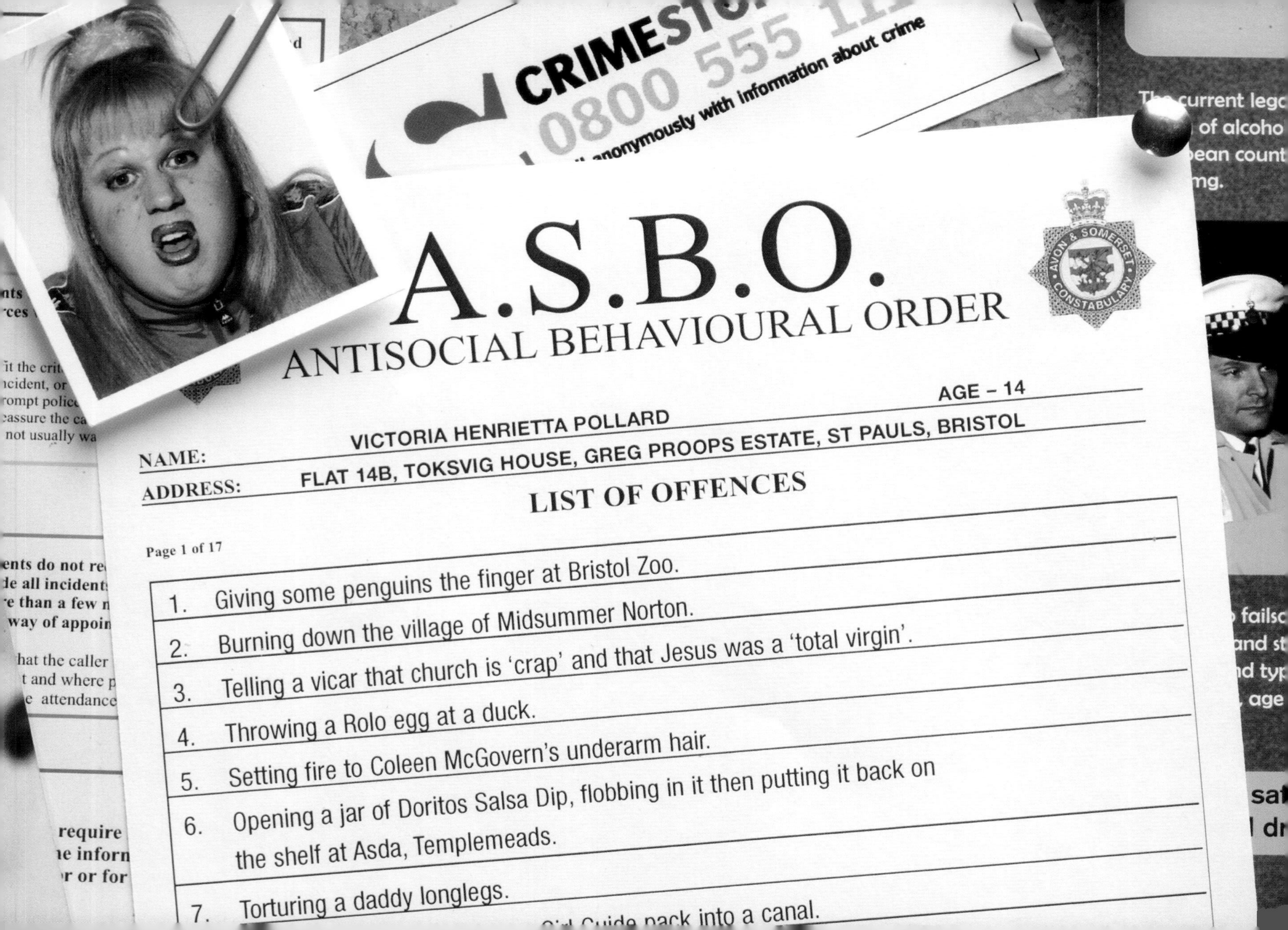

CRIMESTOPPERS
0800 555 111
anonymously with information about crime
A.S.B.O.
ANTISOCIAL BEHAVIOURAL ORDER
AVON & SOMERSET CONSTABULARY
NAME: VICTORIA HENRIETTA POLLARD
AGE – 14
ADDRESS: FLAT 14B, TOKSVIG HOUSE, GREG PROOPS ESTATE, ST PAULS, BRISTOL
LIST OF OFFENCES
Page 1 of 17
1. Giving some penguins the finger at Bristol Zoo.
2. Burning down the village of Midsummer Norton.
3. Telling a vicar that church is 'crap' and that Jesus was a 'total virgin'.
4. Throwing a Rolo egg at a duck.
5. Setting fire to Coleen McGovern's underarm hair.
6. Opening a jar of Doritos Salsa Dip, flobbing in it then putting it back on the shelf at Asda, Templemeads.
7. Torturing a daddy longlegs.

with her eyeliner pencil if he didn't drop her right s—

9.

10. Writing the word 'graffiti', on a wall.

11. Headbutting a squirrel.

12. Telling a judge his wig made him look like 'a complete pervert.'

13. On the way back from the school trip to Wookey Hole, showing the fourth year her own 'Wookey Hole'.

14. Squeezing her spot into Bethany Ray's Chicken Zinger.

15. Giving the lollipop man a wedgy.

16. Biting a dog.

17. Texting several abusive messages to herself.

18. Carving 'this bus is well gay' on the back seat of the D4 bus.

19. Turning up at the opening of the new Bristol City Hospital and giving Her Majesty The Queen 'evils'.

Stealing a train.

P.T.O.

EPISODE two

TOM V/O: Britain, Britain, Britain. Man, it's easily the best goddarn cotton-pickin' country in the world. Yee hah! I went to France; I found it far too French. Spain was full of Spaniards and Poland stank of farts. But what makes Britain so moist and fragrant? Why, it be the people. Let's visit them now. Pack it up, pack it in, let me begin.

LOU AND ANDY — RICHARD AND JUDY

TOM V/O: After a morning spent watching some traffic lights, Lou and Andy are returning home.

EXT: STREET. LOU IS WHEELING ANDY TOWARDS ANDY'S FLAT. LOU STOPS TO CHAT TO A PASSING WOMAN WITH A SMALL CHILD IN A BUGGY.

LOU: Oh hello, how are you? Alright?

LADY: Yeah. Alright?

AS THEY ARE CHATTING ANDY NICKS THE CHILD'S ICE CREAM.

LOU: Keeping well?

LADY: Yeah, I am, thank you. Very good.

LOU: Alright, I'll see you later.

Which one's Richard and which one's Judy?

AS THEY LEAVE, THE LADY LOOKS DOWN AT HER CHILD AND THEN BACK AT LOU AND ANDY, WHO ARE DEPARTING. SHE REALISES WHAT HAS HAPPENED AND COMFORTS THE DISTRESSED CHILD.

INT: ANDY'S FLAT. LOU AND ANDY ARE SAT IN FRONT OF THE TELEVISION, WATCHING *RICHARD AND JUDY*. LOU IS ON THE PHONE.

ANDY: Which one's Richard and which one's Judy?

LOU: (VERY EXCITED, TO ANDY) I can't believe it! I've got through! (ON PHONE) Yes I'll hold. (TO ANDY) Oh my god, it's a thousand pounds a question.

ANDY: Let me do it.

LOU: I'm not sure...

ANDY: I wanna do it.

LOU RELUCTANTLY HANDS THE PHONE TO ANDY.

INT: *RICHARD AND JUDY* STUDIO. ON THE TV SET...

RICHARD: Okay, it's time for 'You Say, We Pay'. And who's on the line?

ANDY: I am.

RICHARD: Sorry, who's there?

Yeah, I know.

ANDY: Andy Pipkin.

JUDY: Hi Andy. You know the rules, don't you. It's very very easy. We show you something and you just have to describe it to us.

ANDY: Yeah, I know.

RICHARD: And for every one that you get right, we give you one thousand pounds.

ANDY: Yeah, I know.

RICHARD: Right, okay then. Well, start the clock, let's go. One minute.

THE CLOCK STARTS. WE SEE A PICTURE OF A CARROT AND THE WORD 'CARROT'.

ANDY: Carrot!

A BUZZER SOUNDS, INDICATING ANDY'S FORFEITED THE QUESTION. RICHARD LOOKS BEHIND.

RICHARD: No, Andy, you have to describe it. You mustn't say what the thing actually is.

ANDY: Yeah, I know.

WE SEE A PICTURE OF MICHAEL PARKINSON.

RICHARD: Okay, let's carry on.

ANDY: Michael Parkinson!

JUDY: No, that is Mike. You don't have to tell us who the person is, you just give us a clue and we guess.

ANDY: Yeah, I know.

WE SEE A PICTURE OF A MOBILE PHONE.

Carrot!

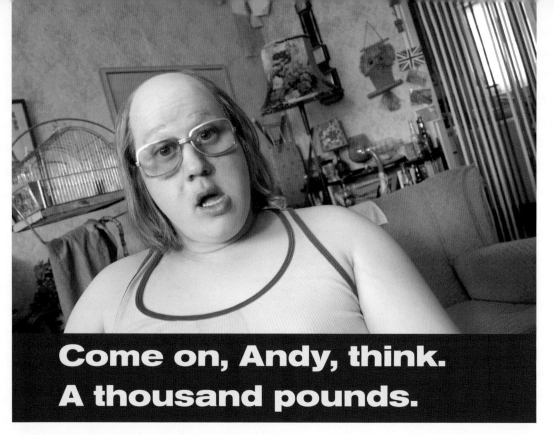

Come on, Andy, think.
A thousand pounds.

ANDY: Mobile phone!

RICHARD AND JUDY BOTH LOOK BEHIND THEM.

RICHARD: Alright, we're running out of time. Let's just try one more quickly, Andy. You just describe it, okay.

WE SEE A PICTURE OF A PINT OF MILK.

ANDY: Er...

LOU: Come on, Andy, think. A thousand pounds.

ANDY: Pint of milk!

LOU SIGHS. ON THE SCREEN...

RICHARD: Oh, we're out of time. Oh, I'm really sorry, mate. You're the first person never to win anything. Oh dear. (MUSIC STARTS) We'll be back after the break.

THE ADVERTS START.

LOU: Oh Andy, why didn't you let me do it?

A CAR ADVERT COMES ON THE TV.

ANDY: Car!

LOU: No, it's finished now. These are just the adverts.

ANDY: Yeah, I know. Laboratoire Garnier!

MRS EMERY — POST OFFICE

TOM V/O: The British postal service is the best in the world. Put a first class stamp on your letter, stick it in a post box and it's guaranteed to possibly arrive at some point somewhere if you're lucky.

INT: POST OFFICE. MRS EMERY IS IN THE QUEUE. AN OLD LADY (IRIS) JOINS THE END OF THE QUEUE. SHE HOLDS HER PENSION BOOK AND HAS A WALKING STICK. BEAT. SHE SPOTS MRS EMERY.

IRIS: Mrs Emery?

MRS EMERY: Oh hallo, dear. How was the operation?

IRIS: Very good. Very good. They had me out in no time.

MRS EMERY: Oh that's good, 'cause the hip's a big one, isn't it?

IRIS: It was a double hip.

MRS EMERY: *Double* hip? Well, you look very well on it. Where did you have it done?

MRS EMERY STARTS PEEING.

IRIS: Um. Oh. At the Queen...

MRS EMERY: Queen Mary?

IRIS: Yes.

MRS EMERY: Yeah, it's good there. They've got very good doctors.

THE QUEUE MOVES UP.

MRS EMERY: Who did you have?

IRIS: Doctor P-p...

MRS EMERY: Doctor Pariedes?

IRIS: Yes.

It's your turn.

MRS EMERY: He did Sheila. You know Sheila Fear. From the chemist.

IRIS: Yes.

WITHOUT NOTICING, MRS EMERY HAS ARRIVED AT THE FRONT OF THE QUEUE.

MRS EMERY: She went in on the Tuesday morning and she was up and about by the weekend.

IRIS: It's your turn.

AS SHE INDICATES THE FREE CASHIER IRIS DROPS HER PENSION BOOK IN THE PEE. MRS EMERY PICKS IT UP.

MRS EMERY: I'll get that for you. You save your hips. Lovely to talk to you. I'll see to you later, dear.

MRS EMERY CARRIES ON PEEING AS SHE WALKS OVER TO THE CASHIER.

MRS EMERY: One second class stamp, please.

VICKY POLLARD – CALL CENTRE

TOM V/O: In Darkley Noone, ASBO enthusiast Vicky Pollard has left half her kids at home as she begins her first day at work.

EXT: STREET. VICKY PUSHES HER SIX-SEAT PUSHCHAIR. SHE COMES TO A HALT OUTSIDE AN OFFICE-STYLE BUILDING.

VICKY: Right, wait there. I'll just be a few hours. (AS SOME OF THE KIDS LOOK AT HER) Don't be givin' me baby evils!

VICKY ENTERS THE BUILDING. HALF A DOZEN OVERWEIGHT, DOWNTRODDEN-LOOKING, BORED WOMEN ARE IN SEPARATE BOOTHS, TALKING ON PHONES. A SEEDY-LOOKING MAN – RON – SHOWS VICKY TO HER SEAT.

RON: It's three pound eighty an hour. Easy work. All you gotta do is talk dirty to 'em.

VICKY: Oh my God, I can so do that 'cause I'm like well a slag.

RON: This is where you sit.

VICKY SITS IN AN EMPTY BOOTH. RON SHOWS HER AN ADVERT IN THE BACK OF THE *SUNDAY SPORT*.

No but yeah but no but yeah this is Spitfire and I'm wearing like really sexy knickers that I got from George at Asda.

RON: Your name is Sapphire. You are six foot tall. You are a top model from Paris. (INDICATES) Bogs over there.

RON AMBLES OFF. THE PHONE RINGS. VICKY IGNORES IT. THE PHONE CONTINUES TO RING.

RON: (RETURNING) Answer the phone!

VICKY: Alright! (IN A POLITE VOICE) Hello, or sumfin' or nuffin'?

WE HEAR THE CALLER. HE HAS A WEST COUNTRY ACCENT.

CALLER: Alright? Is that Sapphire, then?

VICKY: No but yeah but no but yeah this is Spitfire and I'm wearing like really sexy knickers that I got from George at Asda.

What you doin'?

WE SEE THE CALLER – A SEEDY, MIDDLE-AGED MAN, SITTING IN AN ARMCHAIR, WITH A HANDY BOX OF TISSUES NEXT TO HIM.

CALLER: What you doin'?

VICKY: Er, thinking about having a bag of crisps.

CALLER: Oh. You not doin' anything sexy then?

VICKY: Oh no but yeah but no but yeah I am because I'm actually here with three girlfriends who are all like top models and they all do like modelling for the Freeman's catalogue an' that.

CALLER: What are their names?

VICKY: Oh, something really exotic like, um, Ferrero, Rocher and... er... Twix?

CALLER: And what are you all doing?

VICKY: Well, Ferrero is smearing Chambourcey Hippopotamouse all over Rocher.

CALLER: Uhuh. What's Twix doing?

VICKY: Pickin' her feet and watching June Sarpong on *T4*.

CALLER: Pickin' her feet? This is costing me a pound a minute. Can you try and be a bit sexier please?

VICKY: Oh my God I so can't believe you just said that. I am like well the Cotham J-Lo and if Rochelle Atkins says I'm lying then don't listen to her because her brother ate a goldfish for 50p. Anyway, I am like well fit because one time we was all in Media Studies and I was wearing this really short skirt and Mr Jarman who everyone knows is a complete pervert anyway spent the whole lesson totally staring at my Muller Fruit Corner.

CALLER: Vicky?

VICKY: Yeah. Who's this?

CALLER: It's Uncle Pete.

You're not gonna tell Auntie Kath about this, are you?

VICKY: Uncle Pete?! Oh my God, what are you ringing these phone lines for? That is well out of order. Put the phone down!

UNCLE PETE: You're not gonna tell Auntie Kath about this, are you?

VICKY: No, I'm gonna call you back. This is like well costing you a lot.

VICKY PUTS HER PHONE DOWN, PICKS IT UP AGAIN IMMEDIATELY AND DIALS.

UNCLE PETE: Hello?

VICKY: ...So the whole thing is right, we're all covered in Chambourcey Hippopotamouse and we're all like well licking it off each other and I'm like totally lezzing everyone up and... All done? Okay Uncle Pete. I'll see you Sunday. Bye!

DUDLEY AND TING TONG — LADYBOY

INT: DUDLEY'S FLAT/BEDROOM.

TOM V/O: It's five past Ming the Merciless and in Bruise, Dudley and Ting Tong have spent their first night together.

DUDLEY AND TING TONG ARE LYING TOGETHER INTIMATELY. TING TONG BLOWS REPEATEDLY INTO DUDLEY'S EAR TO WAKE HIM. FINALLY, AFTER A REALLY BIG BLOW DUDLEY WAKES.

TING TONG: Are you awake, Mr Dudley?

DUDLEY: Yes, I am. Yes.

TING TONG: Did you have... good time last night?

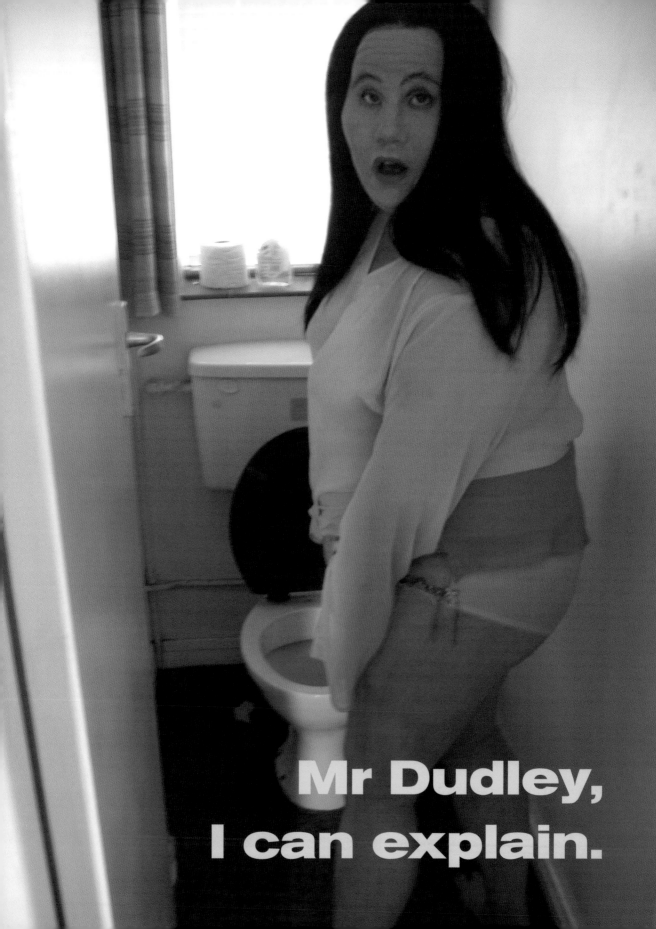

Mr Dudley,
I can explain.

Did you enjoy all these things Ting Tong do for you?

DUDLEY: Yes, it was very pleasant.

TING TONG: Did you enjoy all these things Ting Tong do for you?

DUDLEY: Yes. I did. I found it all to be a wonderful release. Thank you, Ting Tong.

TING TONG: Would you like do it again?

DUDLEY: (PRETENDING TO THINK ABOUT IT) Erm... Yes. That would be most... welcome. Yes.

TING TONG: I just take a little tinkle. Then I return.

TING TONG GETS UP AND EXITS INTO THE ENSUITE.

DUDLEY: (CALLS) Don't be long, cupcake.

TING TONG: Missing you already, Mr Dudley.

WE HEAR WATER BEING PASSED.

DUDLEY: (REMEMBERS) Oh, the flush isn't working. (CALLS THEN GOES AFTER HER) Ting Tong? Ting Tong? The flush isn't...

THE TOILET DOOR IS OPEN. WE SEE THAT SHE IS STANDING UP URINATING.

DUDLEY: No. No. No.

TING TONG: (GASPS) Mr Dudley, I can explain.

DUDLEY: No. No. No. You've got a...

TING TONG: (THROUGH TEARS) I'm sorry Mr Dudley. I was going to tell you.

DUDLEY: When?

TING TONG: After wedding.

DUDLEY: There isn't gonna be a wedding. What are you anyway?

TING TONG: (ASHAMED) I ladyboy.

DUDLEY: You're what?

TING TONG: Yes, Mr Dudley. It time you knew. My real name not Ting Tong. My real name... Tong Ting.

DUDLEY: Get out! Get out of my flat, you ladygayboy!

TING TONG GETS DOWN ON HER KNEES.

TING TONG: I'm sorry, Mr Dudley. I beg of you! Please don't make me leave. Oh, Mr Dudley!

TING TONG STARTS TO CRY AND HUGS HIS LEG. TING TONG'S HEAD IS INADVERTENTLY BY DUDLEY'S GROIN. DUDLEY IS CONFLICTED REMEMBERING LAST NIGHT.

DUDLEY: Maybe you could stay... just one more night.

DUDLEY STROKES TING TONG'S HEAD.

BUBBLES DEVERE — STEAM ROOM

INT: POOL ROOM, LEADING TO STEAM ROOM. DESIREE AND ROMAN ARE HOLDING HANDS.

TOM V/O: At Hill Grange Health Spa, ex-International showjumper Desiree and her husband Roman are making the most of their honeymoon.

ROMAN: I'm very frisky today, my love.

DESIREE: Are you, baby?

ROMAN: Yeah, like a man three quarters of my age.

DESIREE: Well, let's go into the steamy room and have a little bit of hows-your-farthing?

ROMAN CHUCKLES, PATS DESIREE'S AMPLE BEHIND AND THEY GO INTO THE SEEMINGLY EMPTY, VERY STEAMY STEAM ROOM.

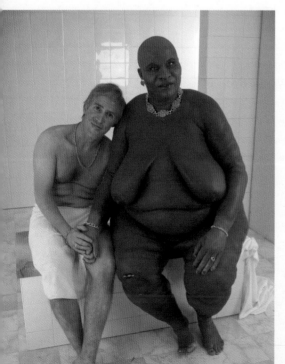

ROMAN: I can show you a thing or two.

DESIREE: I have one or two things to show you...

DESIREE SEDUCTIVELY TAKES OFF HER TOWEL AND SITS ON IT, NEXT TO ROMAN. THEY GO TO KISS.

DESIREE: Oh Roman.

ROMAN: I love you so much.

DESIREE: I love you too, baby.

ROMAN: Just the two of us.

DESIREE: Alone at last.

SUDDENLY A NAKED BUBBLES APPEARS BETWEEN THEM, THROUGH THE STEAM.

BUBBLES: Hello, darlings.

ROMAN: Oh, Bubbles?!

BUBBLES: I trust you are enjoying your honeymoony.

DESIREE: This is so fatiguing to me.

ROMAN: You know, Bubbles, we're trying to have a little bit of private time.

BUBBLES: Oh don't worry about me, darling. I'm so over you, you wouldn't believe it.

DESIREE: Good, 'cause you're never gonna get him back, baby.

BUBBLES: (RAISING VOICE) Well, that's fine by me, I don't want him back after you've had your dirty paws all over him.

DESIREE: How dare you compare me to a bear?!

Oh don't worry about me, darling. I'm so over you, you wouldn't believe it.

DESIREE AND BUBBLES START TUSSLING WITH EACH IN THE STEAM.

BUBBLES: You harlot! You strumpet!

DESIREE: He loves *me* now, you fool!

ROMAN: Ladies, ladies.

THE FIGHT CONTINUES, OBSCURED BY HEAVY STEAM. BUBBLES AND DESIREE SNIPE AND GROWL AT EACH OTHER WITH INDECIPHERABLE SOUNDS. ROMAN IS ENJOYING THE VIEW BUT DECIDES TO INTERVENE.

ROMAN: Please, ladies. Stop!

THE PAIR STOP FIGHTING AND STAND NEXT TO EACH OTHER, GROWLING. WE SEE THAT DESIREE IS BALD BUT FOR A FEW STRANDS OF HAIR. WE SEE BOTH FROM THE WAIST UP ONLY.

ROMAN: Oh, my love. You appear to be missing something.

DESIREE: My necklace?

ROMAN: No.

DESIREE: My earrings? She's taken my earrings!

ROMAN: Um, no. It's your... um...

ROMAN INDICATES TOWARDS DESIREE'S HEAD. DESIREE TOUCHES IT AND REALISES SHE IS BALD.

DESIREE: My wig! She's taken my wig! I didn't even know I wore a wig!

BUBBLES: Don't be ridiculous, darling. I don't have your wig!

DESIREE: (TO ROMAN) Don't just stand there, baby! Help me look for it!

ROMAN: Of course, my sweet.

DESIREE BENDS DOWN TO LOOK ON THE FLOOR, HER GIANT BOTTOM EXPOSED.

BUBBLES: Oh, it's like the black hole of Calcutta!

DESIREE: How dare you make personal remarks about my a-hole?!

ROMAN: Alright, ladies. Now that is enough.

BUBBLES: I'll leave you to it.

DESIREE AND ROMAN CONTINUE TO SEARCH AS BUBBLES LEAVES.

ROMAN: Come on, it must be somewhere.

EXT. STEAM ROOM. BUBBLES EXITS. WE SEE HER FULL-LENGTH FOR THE FIRST TIME SINCE THE FIGHT. SHE IS WEARING DESIREE'S WIG AS A MERKIN AND LAUGHING TRIUMPHANTLY.

BUBBLES: Ha ha ha ha ha ha ha ha!

SHE PASSES GITA, CARRYING A TOWEL.

GITA: Miss Bubble, will you be needing a bikini wax later?

BUBBLES: No thank you, Gita darling. I'm letting it grow!

BUBBLES PASSES ANOTHER MEMBER OF STAFF, WHOSE EYES ARE NATURALLY DRAWN TO BUBBLES'
EXTRAORDINARY BUSH.

BUBBLES: Champagne! Champagne for everyone!

LINDA — MOUSTACHE

INT: LINDA'S OFFICE.

TOM V/O: Meanwhile, in the new town of Dane Bowersville, university lecturer Linda
Flint is busy marking.

LINDA SITS WRITING.

LINDA: (TO HERSELF) This pen is excellent.

THERE'S A KNOCK AT THE DOOR.

LINDA: (CALLS) One moment. (TO HERSELF) Just put the top back on.

LINDA PUTS THE TOP BACK ON THE PEN.

LINDA: Come in.

NINA, A DARK-HAIRED GIRL WITH PRONOUNCED FACIAL
HAIR, ESPECIALLY ON HER TOP LIP, ENTERS.

NINA: Hi Linda.

LINDA: Hello Nina. Take a seat.

NINA DOES SO.

LINDA: What can I help you with today?

NINA: Well, I'm not really enjoying the
Contemporary Womens' Poetry course.
I was wondering if I could change to
Constructions of Sexual Identity in the
Works of Emily Brontë.

Never heard of Immac. **That's right. Magnum PI.**

LINDA: Sounds a bit heavy, but if you're sure.

NINA: Yeah.

LINDA: I'll just check with Martin it's not too late.

LINDA PICKS UP THE PHONE.

LINDA: Martin, it's Linda. I've got a student here who wants to know if she can change courses. It's Nina. You know Nina. Long-flowing skirts, lovely dangly earrings. Looks like she's been slurping a cappuccino. You'd get a stubble rash if you kissed her. Never heard of Immac. That's right. Magnum PI.

SHE COVERS THE PHONE.

LINDA: He says that's fine.

NINA LOOKS UPSET.

NINA: Thanks.

SHE GOES TO EXIT. LINDA RESUMES HER PHONE CALL.

LINDA: Yes, Harriet saw her at the swimming baths. Said it was like Chewbacca in a bikini.

NINA LOOKS BACK AT LINDA. LINDA SMILES, WARMLY.

LINDA: Could you shut the door on your way out?

Yes, Harriet saw her at the swimming baths. Said it was like Chewbacca in a bikini.

EPISODE

MARJORIE DAWES/FATFIGHTERS – DEREK

INT: FATFIGHTERS.

TOM V/O: Why *are* people fat? Because God hates them. So they attend diet classes like this.

THE GROUP ARE CHATTING AMONGST THEMSELVES. SUDDENLY MARJORIE ARRIVES AND IS HOLDING HANDS WITH DEREK, A SPORTY BLACK GUY IN HIS EARLY THIRTIES.

MARJORIE: Hello FatFighters. (TO DEREK) Come 'ere, you.

SHE PULLS DEREK TOWARDS HER AND KISSES HIM. THE GROUP LOOK ON, EMBARRASSED.

Oooh it's a beast.

MARJORIE: (TO DEREK) Later. (TO GROUP) Sorry we're late. I bet you're all wondering who this noooo face is. Well, this sexy MF – hee hee – is Derek, and he's my boyfriend.

DEREK: Yeah, we just met a couple of days ago. Hello everybody.

GROUP: Hello.

MARJORIE: Feels longer though. Feels like I've known you my whole life.

DEREK: (TRYING TO AGREE) Yeah.

MARJORIE: Yeah, we met in the gym. He's a personal trainer.

DEREK: (JOKEY) She was just in the sauna. She wasn't doin' any exercise.

THE GROUP LAUGH.

MARJORIE: I don't just go in the sauna, Derek. I use the sunbed as well. Anyway I'm getting plenty of exercise now, aren't I?

MARJORIE TOUCHES DEREK'S PENIS. DEREK WITHDRAWS A LITTLE, SLIGHTLY EMBARRASSED BUT STILL SMILING.

MARJORIE: Oooh it's a beast.

MARJORIE: So what we're gonna do today is do something a bit different – shake it up a bit – as Derek is gonna get us all up exercising, and we're gonna see if we can't shift a few of them extra stone, eh Pat? (TO DEREK, SOTTO) That's the one I was telling you about. The Walrus.

DEREK: Is she the one who –?

MARJORIE: (POINTING AT TANYA) – no, that's the one who stinks. The old one. (BRIGHTLY) Hi Tanya.

TANYA: (HURT) Hello.

MARJORIE: Oh and I should warn you. That one there is Meera. She is of the Asian persuasion.

DEREK: Hello, Meera.

MEERA: Hello, Derek.

MARJORIE: Not a word. Derek.

DEREK: Okay gang, let's get up on our feet.

I don't just go in the sauna. I use the sunbed as well.

THE GROUP RISE.

DEREK: We'll just start with some stretches.

MARJORIE: You've stretched me. I tell you what, girls. Once you've 'ad black, you ain't going back.

DEREK TRIES TO IGNORE THIS.

DEREK: So I want you to all get into pairs.

THE GROUP DO SO. TANYA IS LEFT ON HER OWN.

TANYA: Oh I haven't got anyone.

DEREK: That's alright, love. You can come with me.

MARJORIE THROWS A LOOK.

TANYA: Oooh!

THE GROUP CHUCKLE ALONG WITH HER. MARJORIE LOOKS DISPLEASED.

DEREK: So I want one of you put a hand on your partner's shoulder to balance, and then lift your leg up behind you and stretch it.

TANYA PUTS HER HAND ON DEREK'S SHOULDER.

PAT: Oooh, you've got lucky there, Tanya.

TANYA: Yeah I know. And he's all muscle.

THE GROUP LAUGH. DEREK SMILES.

MARJORIE: You're flirting again, Derek.

DEREK: I'm just being friendly, Marj. (TO GROUP) Okay, deep breaths everybody. And breathe from the diaphragm, which is here.

DEREK DEMONSTRATES ON TANYA FROM BEHIND.

TANYA: Actually, I wish I were twenty years younger.

GROUP LAUGH.

DEREK: Cheeky.

> You've stretched me. I tell you what, girls. Once you've 'ad black, you ain't going back.

MARJORIE: You're actually very lucky, 'cause I'm not the jealous type, but if you touch that filthy slag again it's over.

TANYA: (WALKING BACK) I was only joking, Marjorie.

MARJORIE: (TO TANYA) And you can shut up an' all, you fat old ugly Lolita!

GROUP SITS DOWN. DEREK STOPS AND APPROACHES MARJORIE. HE TAKES HER TO ONE SIDE.

DEREK: Look I'm not sure me being here's a good idea. I'll call you later.

MARJORIE: Don't bother, you Christopher Casanova! You 'ad me and you lost me. And don't think I'm gonna come running after you because we are through! That's right – screeeeeeeew you!

A BEMUSED DEREK EXITS.

MARJORIE: (REALISING WHAT SHE'S JUST DONE) Just gotta get something out of the car.

MARJORIE TAKES HER SHOES OFF AND RUNS OUT OF THE DOOR.

MARJORIE: (OOV, SCREAMING AND CRYING, VERY DISTRESSED) I'm so sorry. I love you. I need you. Don't leave me. I beg you. Derek. Please, Derek.

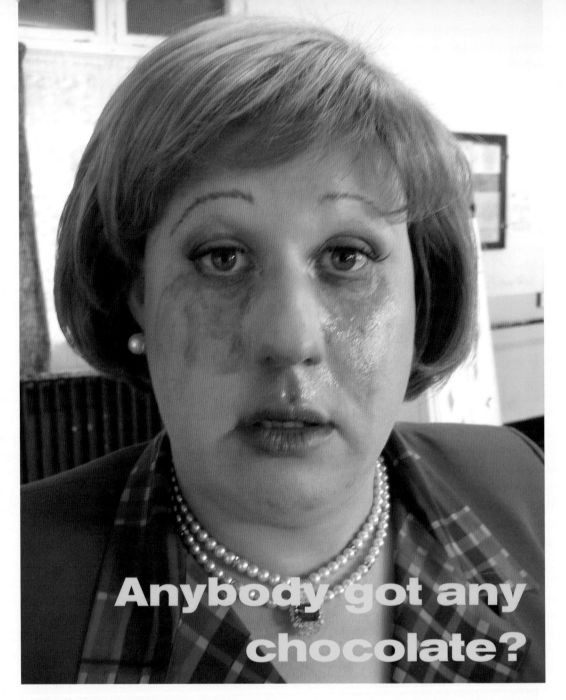

Anybody got any chocolate?

DEREK (OOV) I'm not interested. You're nuts!

MARJORIE: Noooooooo!

WE HEAR A DOOR SLAM AND A CAR PULLS AWAY. A TEARFUL MARJORIE RETURNS, MASCARA RUNNING. SHE IS IN A STATE OF SHOCK BUT IS TRYING TO CONTAIN HERSELF.

MARJORIE: Anybody got any chocolate?

EACH MEMBER OF THE GROUP PULLS OUT A CHOCOLATE BAR FROM THEIR BAGS/POCKETS AND OFFERS IT TO MARJORIE IN UNISON.

LEONARD 1 — MRS CARPENTER

INT: NURSING HOME/LOUNGE. A FEW OLD LADIES ARE SITTING IN ARMCHAIRS AND WATCHING THE TV.

TOM V/O: Old people in Britain are abandoned in homes like this.

MALE NURSE: (LOUDLY) Hello Mrs Carpenter, and how are we today?

MRS CARPENTER: Alright.

MALE NURSE: Right.

THE NURSE TAKES MRS CARPENTER'S CUP OF TEA FROM HER.

MALE NURSE: Let's just get you up out of this chair. There we are, okay?

HE HELPS HER TO HER FEET THEN SETTLES DOWN IN THE ARMCHAIR AND STARTS DRINKING HER TEA.

Let's just get you up out of this chair.

There we are, okay?

DAFYDD – GIRLFRIEND

INT: THE SCARECROW AND MRS KING.

TOM V/O: This is the local pub of out gay man Dafydd Thomas. I thought I might be gay for a while, until I met my lovely wife, Gerald.

MYFANWY IS BEHIND THE BAR. DAFYDD ENTERS. HE IS PO-FACED AND HOLDING HANDS WITH A DOWDY, FAT, PLAIN SPANISH-LOOKING GIRL.

DAFYDD: Hello, Myfanwy. We'd like *two* Bacardi and Cokes, please.

MYFANWY: Coming right up. Who's this?

DAFYDD: This – everybody – is my girlfriend.

MYFANWY: Your girlfriend?

DAFYDD: That's right, Myfanwy. My *girl*friend.

MYFANWY: But you are a gay.

DAFYDD: I know. The only gay in the village, but the people round here are so anti-gayist I have been forced to take myself a girlfriend. (TO EVERYONE) I hope you're happy now!

MYFANWY: So, you won't be having any bumfun at all?

DAFYDD: No Myfanwy. I'm going to be living a lie, tortured by my repressed sexuality. My every waking moment is going to be a misery. For I will never be able to tell her my shameful secret. That I am gay... (IMITATING AN ECHO) gay... gay... homosexual... gay...

MYFANWY: Well, I think she might know by now.

DAFYDD: Oh no, she doesn't speak a word of English.

MYFANWY: What's her name?

DAFYDD: No idea. I don't speak Spanish.

MYFANWY: Well, does she speak Welsh?

DAFYDD: I don't think so. She looked very bored during tonight's episode of *Pobol Y Cwm*.

MYFANWY: Oh, look at her, poor thing.

DAFYDD: I think she was on a rambling tour and got lost.

MYFANWY: (LOUDLY) Are you alright, love?

THE GIRL RATTLES OFF A LONG EXPLANATION IN SPANISH.

DAFYDD: Huh, women!

DAFYDD DOWNS HIS DRINK AND TAKES THE GIRL'S HAND.

DAFYDD: Right. Come along, beard.

MYFANWY: See you later, Dafydd.

DAFYDD AND THE GIRL HEAD FOR THE DOOR.

DAFYDD: Goodbye, Myfanwy. (TO EVERYONE) Well, I hope you people are satisfied. (WITH GREAT SOLEMNITY) My bottom, for now, remains sealed. Thank you.

My bottom, for now, remains sealed. Thank you.

MR MANN – ROY'S PICTURES

EPISODE

INT: ROY'S PICTURES.

TOM V/O: This shop sells paintings. I myself am a great collector of art and have an original at home by Van Gogh. Sally Van Gogh.

ROY STARES AT AN EMPTY SHOP. MR MANN POPS UP.

ROY: Hello.

MR MANN: Hello.

ROY: I did not see you there. Have you been here long?

MR MANN: No, not long. Just about a week or so.

ROY: Right. Can I help you?

MR MANN: I was wondering if you could help me. I am looking to buy a painting of a disappointed horse.

ROY: A disappointed horse?

MR MANN: Yes.

ROY: Well, I'm not sure...

ROY PICKS UP A SELECTION OF PAINTINGS FROM BEHIND HIM.

ROY: How about this one?

MR MANN: That horse looks more peturbed than disappointed.

I was wondering if you could help me. I am looking to buy a painting of a disappointed horse.

ROY: Right. (HE SELECTS ANOTHER) This one?

MR MANN: The horse looks disappointed but not because it received bad news. It looks more like it was disappointed because it had high expectations in life that had remained unfulfilled.

ROY: Now you say it, yes. (HE REVEALS A THIRD PAINTING) How about this one?

MR MANN: I can see the disappointment. I can see the frustration but I can also sense a flicker of hope that things may get better for this horse and that really isn't what I'm looking for.

ROY: One moment.

This one?

ROY STEPS BACK.

MR MANN: Margaret? Margaret?

LONG PAUSE. ROY AND MR MANN EXCHANGE POLITE SMILES.

MARGARET: Yes?

MR MANN: There's a gentleman here wants to know if we have any paintings of a disappointed horse.

MARGARET: Have you shown him the perturbed one, the unfulfilled one and the one that appears disappointed but ultimately has a flicker of hope?

ROY: Yes.

MARGARET: Oh.

ROY: Oh.

MARGARET: Ooh I've got an idea. Roy? Roy?

LONG PAUSE. ROY AND MR MANN BOTH EXCHANGE POLITE SMILES.

ROY: (CALLS) Yes?

MARGARET: If he's looking for pictures of disappointed animals we have a very good one of a vexed kitten.

ROY: Oh, she says we have a very good one of a vexed kitten.

MR MANN: I'm not sure that would make a nice painting. An irked kitten, perhaps, but not vexed.

ROY: Oh, I don't know what to suggest.

MR MANN: Do you have any paintings featuring displeased owls?

ROY: Displeased... Do you know, I think we may have just the thing. (ROY STARES DIRECTLY AT THE PAINTING IN QUESTION) Oh, where did I put it? Oh, here it is.

ROY: Well, what do you reckon?

MR MANN STUDIES IT.

MR MANN: Oh that owl looks very displeased, I will take it.

ROY: Oh I thought we'd never get there.

Oh, I don't know what to suggest.

MR MANN: Yes, I have a painting of an inconvenienced badger at home. I can put it next to that.

ROY: Oh right, did you buy that here?

MR MANN: No, I bought it from the Inconvenienced Badger Painting Shop.

ROY: Oh yes. I know it. How's business?

MR MANN: Slow.

ROY: Right. Well that will be one hundred pounds, please.

MR MANN: (GETTING OUT HIS MONEY) There you go.

THERE IS A MOMENT WHERE THE PAIR DON'T QUITE TRUST EACH OTHER, SO EACH HOLDS ONTO THE THING THEY ARE HANDING OVER FOR A LITTLE TOO LONG. MR MANN GETS AS FAR AS THE DOOR.

MR MANN: I can't help thinking this owl looks more disillusioned than displeased.

ROY: (FLATLY) Get out or I will strangle you.

MR MANN: Goodbye.

MR MANN EXITS.

Get out or I will strangle you.

CURRY 1 – PRAWN VINDALOO

INT: SUBURBAN INDIAN RESTAURANT.

TOM V/O: This couple are visiting their local Indian restaurant. To my mind, anyone who eats foreign food is a traitor and should be shot at dawn.

PAT AND HER HUSBAND DON ARE PERUSING THE MENU. A WAITER STANDS BY.

PAT: I'll have the vegetable biriani, please. That is quite mild, isn't it? And some plain rice.

WAITER: Very good. And for sir?

DON: Might one enquire as to ze spiciest dish upon your menu, my good man?

WAITER: The king prawn vindaloo is very spicy, sir.

DON: Lovely, I'll have one of those, please. (HANDING MENU BACK GRANDLY) Thank you, friend.

PAT: Don, you don't like spicy foods.

DON: Yes, I do.

PAT: You don't.

DON: Woman, I do. I like it spicy. The spicier the better.

THE WAITER APPEARS WITH THE FOOD.

PAT: Ooh, that was quick.

DON: Yeah, it's good service here.

PAT TAKES A BITE.

PAT: Hmm, oh yeah, mine's delicious? How's yours?

DON TAKES A BITE.

DON: Hmm. (PULLS FACE AND WAVES HIS HAND IN FRONT OF HIS MOUTH) Whooh. D-D-D-D-D D-D-D-D-D S Express, Milky Milky. Super match game, super match game, super match game. You are a member of the Rebel Alliance and a spy. I'll have a cuppa tea and a slice of cake, Aunt Sally. (SINGS) The phantom of the opera is here. Inside my mind.

DON TAKES A DRINK OF WATER.

(TO PAT) Bit mild, actually. Super match game!

Hmm. Whooh. D-D-D-D-D D-D-D-D-D S Express, Milky Milky. Super match game, super match game, super match game. You are a member of the Rebel Alliance and a spy. I'll have a cuppa tea and a slice of cake, Aunt Sally. The phantom of the opera is here. Inside my mind.

MAGGIE AND JUDY — HOSPITAL

TOM v/o: In Saint St Anne's hospital, Maggie is recovering from a kidney transplant.

INT: HOSPITAL WARD. THERE ARE SEVERAL OLD LADIES IN HOSPITAL BEDS. ONE OF THEM - IN A MIDDLE BED - IS MAGGIE, READING THE *DAILY MAIL*. JUDY APPEARS, CARRYING SOME GRAPES. SHE SPOTS MAGGIE AND SITS DOWN NEXT TO HER.

JUDY: Hello Maggie.

MAGGIE: Hello dear.

JUDY: How are you today?

MAGGIE: Well, I'm perfectly fine. I told them I'm ready to go home.

JUDY: Now Maggie, you've had a very serious operation. You must listen to the doctors. I've got you these.

JUDY GIVES MAGGIE SOME GRAPES. MAGGIE STUDIES THE STICKER ON THE BAG.

MAGGIE: Oh. South African. I'll have those later.

MAGGIE PUTS THE GRAPES ASIDE. A YOUNG FEMALE DOCTOR – DR DENTON – APPEARS, WITH A CLIPBOARD.

Do you have any other kidneys lying around?

DR DENTON: Mrs... Blackamoor?

MAGGIE: Yes?

DR DENTON: How's the new kidney?

MAGGIE: It's fine, thank you, doctor. I would love to know the name of the donor. I feel I should write to the family and thank them.

DR DENTON: Well, I shouldn't really tell you but I believe it was a Mrs Bannerjee.

MAGGIE STARTS TO FEEL SICK.

JUDY: Maggie?

DR DENTON: Are you alright, Mrs Blackamoor?

Are you alright, Mrs Blackamoor?

MAGGIE VOMITS ALONG THE ROW OF OLD LADIES OPPOSITE. (ONE IS APPLYING SOME MAKE UP, THE MIDDLE ONE IS EATING HER DINNER AND THE THIRD ONE IS SAT UP, ASLEEP, WITH HER MOUTH OPEN.) SHE THEN VOMITS OVER THE DOCTOR. FINALLY SHE PUKES UP HER OWN KIDNEY WHICH A HORRIFIED JUDY CATCHES AND HANDS TO DR DENTON.

MAGGIE: (TO DR DENTON) Do you have any other kidneys lying around?

How's the new kidney?

SEBASTIAN AND MICHAEL — BEAUTIFUL

TOM V/O: It's five past Nicky-nacky-noo-noo and at the Houses of Parliament, *Prime Minister's Questions* is taking place.

INT: HOUSE OF COMMONS. MICHAEL STANDS UP.

MICHAEL: I refer the honourable Member to the answer I gave some moments ago.

MICHAEL SITS DOWN.

SPEAKER: The leader of the opposition.

DAVENPORT STANDS UP.

DAVENPORT: (PLAYFUL) I don't know if the Prime Minister has had an opportunity to view the front page of *The Sun* newspaper today, which shows two photographs of the Prime Minister illustrating how old and tired he looks.

HEARTY LAUGHTER FROM THE OPPOSITION BENCH.

DAVENPORT: Might I suggest that the honourable Member is looking as old and tired as his policies?

MEMBERS JEER.

SPEAKER: Order! Order!

DAVENPORT SITS. THE PM RISES.

MICHAEL: In answer to the honourable gentleman, I have not seen the publication.

THE PM SITS. DAVENPORT RISES.

DAVENPORT: The Prime Minister may be glad to know that I have a copy here.

DAVENPORT PRODUCES A COPY. ON THE COVER ARE TWO PICTURES, SIDE BY SIDE, OF MICHAEL, SHOWING THAT HE HAS AGED BADLY OVER THE PAST FEW YEARS. THEY ARE ACCOMPANIED BY THE HEADLINE 'OAPM'. THERE ARE FURTHER JEERS.

SPEAKER: Order! Order!

EPISODE

Might I suggest that the honourable Member is looking as old and tired as his policies?

'Yes, we are beautiful... no matter what you say... yes, words can't bring us down... no, no, no, no, no... So don't you bring us down, todaaaaaaaa ay-aaaaaay...'

DAVENPORT: Perhaps this is the time for the honourable Member to retire?

CHEERS FROM THE OPPOSITION BENCHES. DAVENPORT SITS. THE PM RISES.

MICHAEL: (FALTERING) This is nothing but a... personal attack on me. My appearance... is not... is not –

MICHAEL IS DISTRACTED BY A DISTANT VOICE, SINGING QUIETLY.

VOICE/ SEBASTIAN: 'You are beautiful, no matter what they say... Words can't bring you down.'

WE SEE SEBASTIAN STEP FORWARD AND APPROACH THE PM.

SEBASTIAN: (GROWING LOUDER) 'Yes, you are beautiful, in every single way... words can't bring you down... so don't you bring me down today.'

MICHAEL GOES TO SPEAK.

MICHAEL: Sebastian –

SEBASTIAN PUTS A FINGER ON MICHAEL'S LIPS.

SEBASTIAN: 'Everyday is so wonderful, then suddenly, it's hard to breathe.'

SEBASTIAN TAKES MICHAEL'S HAND. BEHIND THEM WE SEE A CAMP-LOOKING MP SWOONING AND WAVING A LIGHTER.

SEBASTIAN: ''Cause we are beautiful... no matter what you say... yes, words can't bring us down... no, no, no, no, no... So don't you bring us down, (WALKING BACKWARDS) todaaaaaaaaay -aaaaay...'

SEBASTIAN LEADS MICHAEL BACK TO HIS SEAT.

SEBASTIAN: (SOFTLY) You're beautiful.

SEBASTIAN KISSES MICHAEL ON THE FOREHEAD.

Can we get him working for us?

MICHAEL: Thank you, Sebastian.

SEBASTIAN WALKS OUT PAST EVERYONE, GIVING A WAVE AND MIMING AN 'I'LL CALL YOU LATER' TO ONE OF THE
BACKBENCHERS.

DAVENPORT: (TO SHADOW CHANCELLOR) Can we get him working for us?

LOU AND ANDY — BOAT TRIP

TOM V/O: Lou and Andy are sailing down the River Thames. The Thames was
modelled on the opening credits of EastEnders.

EXT: RIVER THAMES. LOU AND ANDY ARE AMONGST A SMALL GROUP OF JAPANESE TOURISTS ON A SIGHTSEEING BOAT.

LOU: So that was the old GLC building, and in a few minutes we'll be approaching the
Thames Barrier, which was built in 1982 to protect the city from the risk of flooding.

ANDY: This is boring.

LOU: But you've been wanting to come on this boat trip for ages. You always said the
only way to see London was via its ancient waterway, which was like a pulsating artery
through the heart of this historic city.

But you've been wanting to come on this boat trip for ages. You said the only way to see London was via its ancient waterway, which was like a pulsating artery through the heart of this historic city.

YEAH, I KNOW.

ANDY: Yeah, I know.

LOU: Well then?

ANDY: Boring.

LOU: (SIGHS) Would a choc-ice make any difference?

ANDY: Maybe.

LOU: Alright. I'll go and get you a choc-ice then.

LOU EXITS AND GOES DOWN SOME STAIRS, OUT OF VIEW. ANDY GETS UP AND EXITS SHOT. LOU RETURNS WITH TWO CHOC-ICES TO FIND AN EMPTY WHEELCHAIR. HE LOOKS ROUND, CONCERNED.

LOU: Yeah, that's a nice choc-ice, that one, yes... Andy? Andy?! Where are you?

CUT TO : EXTREME WIDE SHOT OF THE BOAT, FROM THE RIVERBANK. ANDY IS WATERSKIING OFF THE BACK OF THE BOAT. WE CAN JUST MAKE OUT LOU, ON THE DECK OF THE BOAT, WANDERING AROUND LOOKING FOR HIM, TO NO AVAIL.

LOU: Andy? Andy?

TOM V/O: And so we conclude our journey round Little Britain. If you have found this show in any way distasteful, and wish to make a complaint, please write to the Chuckle Brothers, care of the CBBC. Good sigh!

EPISODE

SUNSEARCHERS
INTERNATIONAL TRAVEL AGENCY

SIBERIA Camping Holiday £219

Carol Beer's Holiday Hotspots!

'Hello folks, it's Carol here from SunSearchers holidays. Now I pride myself on being a very adventurous free spirit – sometimes I just move my holepunch on my desk for no reason and I'm just the same when it comes to holidays!

Are you looking to go somewhere a bit different for your holiday this holiday? Are you bored of Venice, of all those canals and boats and that? Does the thought of joining the millions of partygoers at the world-famous carnival in Rio de Janeiro sound a bit tedious? Are you filled with dread at the idea of going to Egypt and trekking across the desert just to look at another shitting pyramid?

Well today computer says YES – because you can take a break from the norm (as they said in that hilarious advert for twixes bars) and try one of Carol's holiday hotspots.'

Who needs Disneyland when you've got Newport Pagnell Services?

There's plenty for the kiddies to do. They can either play on the fruit machine or look at a wall, and for mum there's a toilet. If you're hungry, why not buy a packet of Polos from the shop (that sells Polos)?
Week, full board for four – £68 per person (sleep in own car)

If, like me, you're partial to muddy hole, why not spend time in this ditch in Belgium

It's got everything you could want from a ditch – a couple of inches of water, grassy sides and a bad, rotting smell – a bit like eggs or poo. Forget the Grand Canyon, this is the bollocks.
Week, self-catering, £79 per perse

3

Forget the Metropolitan in London – all the celebs like, I dunno, Kerry Katona from OK! magazine or that man in that show I like, hang out here, in this bin, round the back of Morrisons in Hull.

It's got everything you could want from a bin and more! Thursdays are the happening nights here – the management operate a guest list so book early. **Week, half-board, £190 per person.** Happy star-spotting!

4

If you like watersports (and I don't mean being urinated on for sexual gratification) then why not book a break at the Aberystwyth swimming baths.

It's like the Great Barrier Reef only nearer. There are two pools – the main one, which has lots to see under the surface, including plasters, verucca socks and hair, and there's a baby pool too, which is lovely and warm, because the children wee in it.

There's also a table-tennis table (but there's only one bat) and for the foodies, there's a cafe with an extensive manu offering jacket potato with two fillings – beans or plain. There's also a vending machine stocking out-of-date packs of Payne's Poppets, though when I tried it I put the money in and nothing came out.

Week, fly-drive, £249 per person

5

Strictly for the Shopaholic!!!

So you've been to the markets in Marrakech and you've shopped til you've dropped on Rodeo Drive (re-enacting the famous scene from the Richard Gere/Julia Roberts film 'Pretty Lady'). Now it's time to sample the delights of Ron's Kiosk at Chippenham Station. It's got everything you could ever want to buy, from newspapers to cough sweets and grotmags. Book early to avoid disappointment.
Week, £86 per person. Timeshare option available.

Happy Holidays!
I hate you all. *Carol Beer*

EPISODE *three*

TOM V/O: Britain, Britain, Britain. There's so much to see and do here. Why not get stuck in the one-way system in Birmingham or get caught up in a fight in a pub car park in Swansea? Or why not get food poisoning from a motorway service café just outside Stoke? But our greatest attraction is the people of Britain. Hip hop, don't stop.

VICKY POLLARD – ROASTING

TOM V/O: It's early late afternoon morning, and this is the office of PR guru Cliff Maxford.

INT: SWANKY OFFICE. WE SEE A SIGN – 'CLIFF MAXFORD PR LTD'.

CLIFF: Take a seat. Now, I've spoken to the *News Of The World*. They are *very* interested in your story. What happened?

VICKY: What happened was was I met all these footballers and I got like totally roasted. Can I have a thousand hundred pounds now please?

VICKY HOLDS OUT HER HANDS.

CLIFF: First we need to establish this is a genuine story. Now, let's start at the beginning.

CLIFF TAKES NOTES.

VICKY: We was all up this club called Chinese Whites and there was all these famous people there like Dean Gaffney and Jodie Marsh and fingy, you know, that Professor Stephen Hawkings and it was amazing and I'm like well the fittest girl there and loads of people came in from *Coronation Street* and they was all, like, trying to do me, even that little one Chesney was trying to stick his tongue down my throat but I'm not a slag or nuffin'. I wanna find a proper life partner cos I've already had six kids by seven different blokes.

Can I have a thousand hundred pounds now please?

CLIFF: So when did you meet the footballers?

VICKY: I'm getting there! God, I was just about to say it if you had just wai-ted. Then all the footballers came in or somefin or nuffin from all the clubs like Tottenham and Spurs and Chelsea Park Rangers and they all like really wanted to do me but I was wearing this really short skirt – so they could all see my Strawberry Mivvi.

CLIFF: What happened next?

VICKY: Then all the footballers took back me to this really amazing expensive hotel called Travelodge and I thought it was just to talk about football but then I ended up doin' sex with all of 'em but afterwards I felt really used because I thought they all loved me.

CLIFF: Have you got any photographic evidence?

VICKY: No but yeah but no but yeah but I actually have actually so shut up because this is a actual photo from it.

I was wearing this really short skirt – so they could all see my Strawberry Mivvi.

VICKY PULLS OUT A PICTURE SHE HAS DRAWN OF HER IN A BED. IN IT ARE LOTS OF STICK MEN WITH THE HEADS OF FOOTBALLERS THAT SHE HAS STUCK ON E.G. DAVID BECKHAM, WAYNE ROONEY, THIERRY HENRY, SVEN GORAN ERIKKSON AND A BLACK AND WHITE PHOTO OF BOBBY CHARLTON.

VICKY: There's me there actually doin' it with all of them. God I feel so degraded and used and dirty and it was rubbish anyway cos they all had well tiny knobs.

CLIFF: (WEARY) Vicky, I'm not sure this story's gonna stick.

VICKY: Oh my God, I so can't believe you just said that. I am like well gonna be the new Abi Titchmarsh.

CLIFF: (STANDS) Please Vicky, I'm a very busy man.

CLIFF GETS UP TO SHOW HER OUT.

CLIFF: Come back when you've got a better story.

CLIFF GETS RID OF VICKY AND CLOSES THE DOOR. IMMEDIATELY THERE IS A KNOCK ON THE DOOR.

CLIFF: Yes?

VICKY: I done a gang bang with G4.

CLIFF ROLLS HIS EYES AND SHUTS THE DOOR IN HER FACE.

I done a gang bang with G4.

LOU AND ANDY – BREASTS

EXT: STREET.

TOM V/O: It's a quarter to Gino Ginelli and Lou has been out shopping for his friend Andy.

LOU APPROACHES ANDY'S FLAT. HE CARRIES SOME HEAVY SHOPPING BAGS. HE DROPS ONE OF THEM AND THE CONTENTS SPILL ONTO THE FLOOR. A NICE OLD LADY STOPS AND HELPS HIM PICK THINGS UP. THE FINAL ITEM SHE PICKS UP IS A COPY OF *RAZZLE*.

LOU: It's not for me. It's for a disabled man.

DISGUSTED, SHE HANDS IT TO HIM AND WALKS OFF.

INT: ANDY'S FLAT. ANDY IS SAT IN PYJAMAS WATCHING *MONSTER TRUCKS* AND EATING BREAKFAST CEREAL FROM THE BOX.

ANDY: (FLAT) Come on yellow truck.

WE HEAR KEYS IN THE DOOR. LOU ENTERS WITH HIS SHOPPING.

LOU: Morning, Andy.

ANDY: Morning, Len.

LOU: Lou.

ANDY: Yeah, I know.

LOU: I got all your shopping for you.

ANDY: Did you get me *Razzle*?

No, I want that one and that one.

LOU: (DISAPPROVING) Yes. (HANDING THE MAGAZINE OVER) But I don't want you to spend the whole day looking at pictures of naked ladies.

ANDY STUDIES THE MAGAZINE. HE POINTS.

ANDY: I want that one and that one.

You want breasts?

LOU: Well, we'd all like a go on a nice naked lady, yes.

ANDY: No, I want that one and that one.

LOU: You want breasts?

ANDY: Yeah.

LOU: You want a breast enlargement operation?

ANDY: Yeah.

LOU: Why?

ANDY: Summat to play with.

LOU: I'm not sure that's a good idea.

ANDY: I want tits.

LOU: It'd be a right kerfuffle and anyway I thought you were against plastic surgery. I thought you said that cosmetic enhancement was symptomatic of a sick society that worships a cult of youth and beauty, and that anyone seeking the quick fix of physical change was left morally wanting.

ANDY: Yeah, I know.

LOU: Well then.

ANDY: Want tits, though.

LOU: Oh, for the love...

EXT: HOSPITAL. LOU WHEELS ANDY OUT. ANDY HAS A LARGE PAIR OF BREASTS BENEATH HIS VEST.

ANDY: I look a pillock.

LOU SIGHS AND WHEELS ANDY BACK INTO THE HOSPITAL.

It'd be a right kerfuffle and anyway I thought you were against plastic surgery. I thought you said that cosmetic enhancement was symptomatic of a sick society that worships a cult of youth and beauty, and that anyone seeking the quick fix of physical change was left morally wanting.

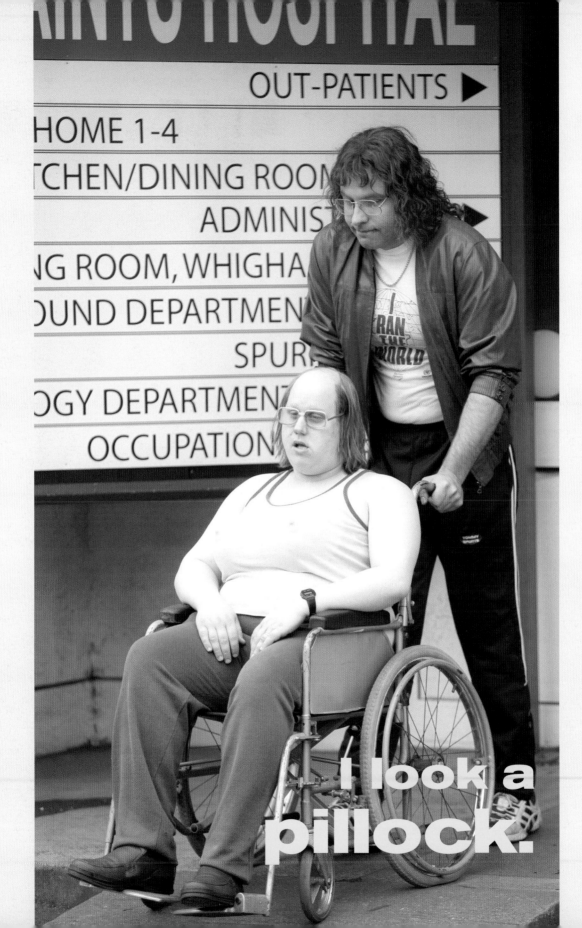

ANNE – RESTAURANT

TOM V/O: Our next stop is at this charming restaurant just off the A27390938662... 5.

INT: EVENING. PLUSH RESTAURANT, WHICH IS FAIRLY BUSY. DR LAWRENCE AND DR BEAGRIE ARE SAT AT A TABLE.

DR LAWRENCE: The reason I've brought you here today is because one of our patients, Anne – have you met Anne? – well, she's got herself a job here as a pianist. It's just a part-time job but she does find playing the piano very calming.

DR BEAGRIE NODS. ANNE ENTERS FORMALLY, CLEARS HER THROAT, STRETCHES HER FINGERS, AND SITS DOWN, BACK STRAIGHT. THERE IS A SMATTERING OF POLITE APPLAUSE, WHICH SHE ACKNOWLEDGES WITH A NOD. ANNE STARTS TO PLAY PROPERLY THEN BEGINS TO THUMP THE KEYS DISCORDANTLY.

ANNE: Eh-eh-eh.

DR LAWRENCE: It must be one of her own compositions.

ANNE TAKES OFF HER SLIPPER AND STARTS TO WHACK THE KEYS.

ANNE: Eh-eh-eh.

ANNE THEN HURLS THE SLIPPER ACROSS THE ROOM. IT LANDS IN DR BEAGRIE'S SOUP, SPLASHING HIM DRAMATICALLY.

DR LAWRENCE: Ooh, careful. There's a slipper in your soup.

ANNE WALKS OVER TO DR. BEAGRIE. SHE LIFTS HER SKIRT TO HIS FACE. WHEN HE DOESN'T REACT SHE PICKS UP HER SLIPPER AND WALKS OFF.

ANNE: (TO THE ROOM) Thank you very much, you've been a wonderful audience.

> **Thank you very much, you've been a wonderful audience.**

EPISODE

CAROL – CRUISE

EXT: 'SUNSEARCHERS' TRAVEL AGENTS. WE SEE CAROL BEER INSIDE THE SHOP, STANDING AT THE WINDOW. SHE PINS UP A POSTER THAT READS 'BAGHDAD - £149 - KIDS GO FREE'.

TOM V/O: Holidays can be booked at travel agents like this. The word "holiday" is derived from the Greek word, "holidius", which directly translates as "sex with coach driver".

INT: TRAVEL AGENTS. CAROL BEER IS SAT AT HER DESK. AN ELDERLY COUPLE - HOWARD AND HILDA - ARE ABOUT TO SIT DOWN IN FRONT OF HER.

CAROL: Could I just finish my coffee?

Are you under sixteen?

HOWARD: Yes.

CAROL: (CALLS) Sue? Can you make me a cup of coffee?

CAROL NODS POLITELY AT THE COUPLE. AFTER A WHILE, HER COFFEE ARRIVES. SHE BLOWS ON IT AND DRINKS IT. SHE SEEMS TO HAVE FINISHED IT BUT SHAKES THE MUG A LITTLE AND FINISHES IT OFF.

CAROL: That was foul. Do take a seat.

THE BEMUSED PAIR SIT DOWN.

HOWARD: We've got our golden wedding anniversary coming up.

HILDA: Yes, we'll have been married fifty years in August.

CAROL SHRUGS.

HOWARD: We've been saving up and we've always promised ourselves a cruise.

HILDA: Maybe something with Saga.

CAROL TYPES.

CAROL: Computer says no.

All the pickled herring you can eat.

HOWARD: Oh.

CAROL: It gets booked up early, you see. Old people.

HILDA: Oh.

CAROL: I've got another option. P & O.

HILDA: Oooh.

HOWARD: Where does that go?

CAROL: Dover to Calais.

HILDA: No, we're looking for a proper cruise.

CAROL: I've got a good deal here.

HOWARD: Yes?

CAROL: There's a Russian cargo vessel taking nuclear waste to the Baltic.

HOWARD: I really don't fancy that.

CAROL: All the pickled herring you can eat.

HILDA: Um, no.

CAROL: No.

CAROL TYPES.

CAROL: Do you have to be in a cruise ship or could you be in a canoe?

HILDA: We're not keen on canoeing.

CAROL: Shame, I've got some great deals here on PGL adventure holidays. Are you under sixteen?

HOWARD: No.

CAROL: No.

HOWARD: We'll leave it then. Thank you.

THE PAIR GO TO LEAVE. HILDA COUGHS AS SHE GETS UP.

CAROL: Can you put your hand over your mouth when you cough, please? That's disgusting!

HILDA: Sorry.

CAROL COUGHS IN HER FACE.

There's a Russian cargo vessel taking nuclear waste to the Baltic.

DUDLEY AND TING TONG — TRIVIAL PURSUIT

INT: DUDLEY'S FLAT/LIVING ROOM.

TOM V/O: Trivial Pursuit is Britain's second most popular board game, after Poke Mummy.

DUDLEY AND TING TONG ARE SAT PLAYING TRIVIAL PURSUIT.

DUDLEY PICKS A CARD.

DUDLEY: People and Places.

DUDLEY: Ooh, this is a hard one for you. 'Who replaced Lord Carrington as Britain's Foreign Secretary during the Falklands War?'

TING TONG: Francis Pym.

DUDLEY: (AMAZED) Correct. How did you know that?

TING TONG: Well, in my little village of Pong Pong we do have plenty newspaper.

DUDLEY: Yes, well, piece of pie for you.

TING TONG ROLLS AGAIN. SHE LANDS ON ENTERTAINMENT. DUDLEY PICKS A CARD.

TING TONG: Pink.

DUDLEY: Ooh, you'll never get this one. 'What was *BBC Breakfast* fitness queen Diana Moran better known as?' I used to have quite a thing for her.

TING TONG: The Green Goddess. 'Nother go.

DUDLEY: Hang on a sec. If you lived your whole life in Pong Pong, Ting Tong, how did you know about the Green Goddess?

TING TONG: Um. Well...

DUDLEY: Where exactly are you from, Ting Tong?

TING TONG: Ting Tong from Tooting.

DUDLEY: Tooting, Ting Tong, not Pong Pong?!

TING TONG: Tooting not Pong Pong for Ting Tong.

Yes, well, piece of pie for you.

DUDLEY: Lies upon lies upon deceit upon lies!

TING TONG: I'm sorry, Mr Dudley.

DUDLEY: (STANDS): Come on! Get out! Get out of my flat!

TING TONG: But Mr Dudley –

DUDLEY: That's it! Pack your bags! I want you out!

DUDLEY USHERS HER INTO THE BEDROOM. HE WAITS OUTSIDE THE ROOM.

TING TONG: (CALLS) Is that it, then? Six wonderful days, over just like that?

DUDLEY: Yes, over.

TING TONG: (CALLS) Is there nothing I can do?

Hello. I Green Goddess. I here to get you up in the morning.

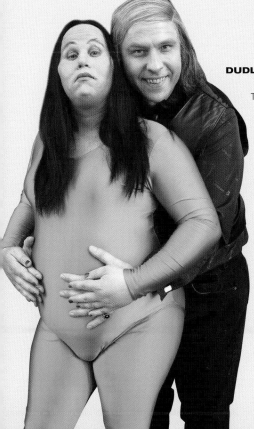

DUDLEY: Nothing. Nothing at all.

THE DOOR OPENS. TING TONG APPEARS, IN A TIGHT-FITTING GREEN LEOTARD.

TING TONG: Hello. I Green Goddess. I here to get you up in the morning.

DUDLEY: (AROUSED) Oh God.

TING TONG: You still want me go?

DUDLEY: Not just yet.

TING TONG DISAPPEARS BACK INTO THE ROOM, LEADING DUDLEY BY HIS TIE, AND SHUTS THE DOOR.

TING TONG: (FROM THE BEDROOM) Now, first let's go do warm-up.

SIR NORMAN FRY – HAMPSTEAD HEATH

EXT: COUNTRY ESTATE.

TOM V/O: It's half past Top Cat, the indisputable Boss Cat, and MP Sir Norman Fry is once again facing the press.

SIR NORMAN FRY, HOLDING HANDS WITH HIS WIFE CAMILLA AND THEIR TWO YOUNG CHILDREN, APPROACHES THE GATE AT THE END OF THE DRIVE. A LARGE GROUP OF JOURNALISTS, PHOTOGRAPHERS AND TV CREWS ARE PRESENT. SIR NORMAN HAS HIS ARM AROUND CAMILLA, WHO LOOKS TEARFUL BUT IS PUTTING ON A BRAVE FACE. THE CHILDREN LOOK EMBARRASSED. SIR NORMAN TAKES OUT A PIECE OF PAPER.

PRESS: Sir Norman! Sir Norman! Will you be resigning?

SIR NORMAN: I have a statement I would like to read. On Monday night, following a long meeting with the Chancellor, I needed to go to the toilet, so I went to one that I knew would be open at three in the morning, on Hampstead Heath. Upon my arrival I met two men – Carlos and Eduardo – who invited me into their cubicle to talk to them about government policy. Unfortunately, I slipped on the wet floor and became sandwiched between the two men in a position that the arresting officer informed me is known as a spit roast.

THE SON TURNS TO ASK HIS MOTHER SOMETHING. THE MOTHER GESTURES TO SAY 'I'LL TELL YOU LATER'.

SIR NORMAN: As far as I am concerned that is the end of the matter. (PAUSE) And by the way, Carlos, if you've had the x-ray and found my watch, please do return it to me. It belonged to my late father. Thank you.

SIR NORMAN GOES TO KISS HIS WIFE FOR THE CAMERAS. SHE PROFFERS A CHEEK. JOURNALISTS CLAMOUR TO ASK MORE QUESTIONS.

...I slipped on the wet floor and became sandwiched between the two men in a position that the arresting officer informed me is known as a spit roast.

MARJORIE DAWES/FATFIGHTERS — CHARLIE SLATER

INT: FATFIGHTERS. THE USUAL GROUP ARE PRESENT, AS WELL AS ONE NEW FACE, THE ACTOR DEREK MARTIN.

TOM V/O: These are amongst the few fat people left in Britain, after Her Majesty the Queen ordered a cull in her Jubilee year. God bless you, ma'am.

MARJORIE: ...also tried something new, dust on a stick. Now, you may have noticed that we have a nooo face in our midstssss. He is a noooo member and he is actually a very famous ac-tor. Now we've had a word. He wants to lose a few pounds but he don't want to be treated any different. So would you please welcome... from *EastEnders*... Charlie Slater!

MARJORIE APPLAUDS WILDLY. THE OTHERS APPLAUD POLITELY. DEREK MARTIN NODS, A LITTLE EMBARRASSED.

DEREK: Thank you.

MARJORIE: Oh, I'm sorry. I called you Charlie, didn't I, love? What's your real name my sweet?

DEREK: Derek. Derek Martin.

MARJORIE: So Charlie, welcome to the group.

ALL: Hello.

MARJORIE: Stop bothering him. Honestly, he's not even one of the main ones. So Charlie, what we do with all nooo members is we weigh them. So do you just wanna pop up on to the scales for me, my love?

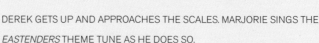

He's here because he's very fat so let's not embarrass him.

DEREK GETS UP AND APPROACHES THE SCALES. MARJORIE SINGS THE *EASTENDERS* THEME TUNE AS HE DOES SO.

MARJORIE: No, don't because he's not here because of that. He's here because he's very fat so let's not embarrass him.

DEREK GETS ON THE SCALES.

MARJORIE: So you are – actually I must just ask you, I never watch it myself - but what's gonna happen with Kat and Alfie? Is their marriage gonna survive the affair? Is he gonna leave her?

DEREK: Look, I'm just here really to try and lose some weight.

MARJORIE: (LOUDLY) Yeah he's on telly. Get over it. (TO DEREK) I know exactly what it's like being famous. Because I've actually been in the audience on *The Wright Stuff*. So you are sixteen stone five. D'you know, that surprises me because you're fat but on telly you look really fat. Really grotesque.

DEREK: Thanks very much.

MARJORIE: My pleasure. Off you pop.

A BEMUSED DEREK DOES SO.

MARJORIE: Give him room! Now, today we're gonna be looking at calorie hotsp– (TO DEREK) Actually, I must just ask... have you got Nigel Harman's phone number for me, ha ha?

DEREK: I don't think Nigel would want me to give it out.

MARJORIE: God, Nigel Harman, eh, girls? Eh? Phwoar! We like a bit o' Nigel, don't we? Eh? Phwoar. I would let him do some really grim stuff to me. Eh? Nigel Harman? Yeah? NIGEL! (GETTING CARRIED AWAY) We like a bit o' Nigel, don't we? Yeah? (SHOUTING AND SHAKING) Yeah! Nigel? Nigel! YEAH? NIGEL! Sorry, Meera here probably doesn't have a clue what I'm talking about.

MEERA: Yes, *EastEnders*. I love it.

MARJORIE: No, I can't... Do it again.

MEERA: I love it.

We like a bit o' Nigel, don't we?

MARJORIE: No... Do it again.

MEERA: I love it.

MARJORIE: Do it again.

MEERA: I love it.

MARJORIE: Oh, right! No, do it again.

MEERA: I love it.

MARJORIE: *EastEnders*, Meera. It's like The Mahabharat only shorter. (TO ALL) So, the thing about calories is – actually, I must just ask – what happens to Mo in the end?

DEREK: I don't know what you mean.

MARJORIE: Well, what happens to her in the end?

DEREK: Well, I don't know. We're not really told that.

MARJORIE: Oh, but what happens to Pauline in the end?

DEREK: Dunno.

MARJORIE: What happens to Phil in the end?

DEREK: I don't know.

MARJORIE: What happens to Dot in the end?

DEREK: Look. These things, I dunno, they haven't been decided yet.

MARJORIE: No, but what happens to Ian in the end?

DEREK: There isn't really an end. It just kind of carries on.

MARJORIE: What happens to Sonia in the end?

DEREK: Look, I don't know! I don't know what happens to any of these people! Stop asking me what happens to all these people in the end!

MARJORIE: What happens to Pat in the end?

DEREK: Look, I'm sorry (HE STANDS) but I just come here to lose some weight. I didn't really need it to be a whole thing about being in *EastEnders*. I've obviously made a mistake. I'm sorry, alright?

DEREK LEAVES. SILENCE. MARJORIE TURNS TO THE GROUP. SHE DOES THE *EASTENDERS* DRUM ROLL.

DEREK: Give it a rest.

MARJORIE: (TO THE GROUP) Shame on you.

LETTY – BIRTHDAY

TOM V/O: In Slut, Letty Bell is celebrating her birthday. Look at them. What a lot of old trouts.

INT: TWEE HOUSE. LIVING ROOM. WE ARE SURROUNDED BY FROG PARAPHERNALIA. THERE ARE GREEN BALLOONS AND FROGGY BIRTHDAY BANNERS. AN EXCITED LETTY IS JOINED BY THREE OLD WOMEN. IN FRONT OF LETTY IS A FROGGY BIRTHDAY CAKE WITH GREEN CANDLES.

GROUP: (SINGS)
'Happy birthday to you,
Happy birthday to you,
Happy birthday dear Letty,
Happy birthday to you'.

I love me froggies, me.

LETTY BLOWS THE CANDLES OUT, ACCIDENTALLY SPITTING ALL OVER THE CAKE AS SHE DOES SO. APPLAUSE.

LETTY: Ah, a lovely froggy cake as well. Shame to cut it, really.

EVIE: We know you love your froggies.

LETTY: I love me froggies, me. I don't know why but I do.

EVIE: Actually all of us clubbed together to get something special.

LETTY: Ooh, something special. A special something. What's that then?

THERE ARE SMILES OF ANTICIPATION FROM THE GROUP AS LETTY IS HANDED A LARGE PARCEL, WRAPPED IN FROGGY WRAPPING PAPER.

LETTY: Ooh, that's a big one ha ha ha. What is it?

EVIE: Open it and find out.

LETTY: Yes, I'll find out when I open it, yeah.

LETTY OPENS THE PRESENT. WE SEE THAT IT IS A LARGE GLASS TANK WITH SOME FOLIAGE AND A REAL FROG IN IT.

LETTY: What's that?

Help yourself to cake.

EVIE: It's a real frog.

LETTY: Urgh!

LETTY RECOILS BACK FROM THE TANK.

DAISY: It won't hurt you.

MILLIE: It's nothing to be scared of. Look, he's lovely. Go on. Give him a stroke.

MILLIE TAKES THE FROG AND PROFFERS IT TOWARDS LETTY.

PAUSE. THE OTHERS LOOK ON, SMILING. LETTY GINGERLY GOES TO TOUCH IT, THEN KNOCKS IT VIOLENTLY OUT OF MILLIE'S HANDS ONTO THE FLOOR.

LETTY: It bit me!

MILLIE: No it didn't.

LETTY: It bit me with its sharp frog teeth! Get it out! Get it out the house!

LETTY HURRIES TO THE SIDEBOARD.

DAISY: We'll have to take it back.

MILLIE: I thought she liked them.

LETTY RETURNS WITH A ROLLING PIN.

LETTY: Stand back!

SHE KNEELS DOWN AND STARTS TO BLUDGEON AND THEN ROLL THE FROG. SHE DOES THIS A FEW TIMES. THE LADIES LOOK ON, HORRIFIED.

LETTY: Help yourself to cake.

MORE BLUDGEONING AND ROLLING. SHE THEN PICKS UP THE FLATTENED FROG AND HURLS IT ACROSS THE ROOM. IT LANDS FLAT ON THE WINDOW AND SLIDES SLOWLY DOWN, LEAVING A TRAIL OF GREEN SLIME BEHIND IT.

LETTY: Still, lovely froggy wrapping paper. I can use that again.

Still, lovely froggy wrapping paper.

BUBBLES DEVERE — MASSAGE

EXT: HILL GRANGE HEALTH SPA.

TOM V/O: At Hill Grange Health Spa, former Miss Botswana Desiree DeVere is relaxing after her fried onion foot scrub.

DESIREE IS SEATED WITH ANOTHER LARGE WOMAN READING A MAGAZINE.

DESIREE: Oh, hasn't that Victoria Beckham put on weight? She looks grotesque.

WOMAN: (AGREEING) Oh yes.

BUBBLES PASSES BY IN THE BACKGROUND.
SHE SPOTS DESIREE AND QUICKENS HER STEP.

INT: HILL GRANGE HEALTH SPA/TREATMENT ROOM.
ROMAN IS BEING GIVEN A FACIAL BY GITA. HE HAS A TOWEL OVER HIS MIDDLE, A GREEN FACEMASK ON AND CUCUMBER PIECES OVER HIS EYES.

GITA: What I'm using is a green algae mask, because your skin is quite sensitive.

ROMAN: Yes that's lovely, it's very soothing.

AT THIS POINT THE DOOR OPENS AND BUBBLES SLIPS IN, WITH A FINGER OVER HER MOUTH.

BUBBLES: Sssssh.

SHE APPROACHES A QUIZZICAL GITA, GIVES HER A FIVE POUND NOTE AND USHERS HER OUT.

ROMAN: Everything alright, Gita?

> # Oh, hasn't that Victoria Beckham put on weight? She looks grotesque.

BUBBLES: (ATTEMPTING JAPANESE ACCENT) Oh yes, everything's fine darling, I mean Mr DeVere. And now I give you massage.

SHE STARTS TO MASSAGE ROMAN'S LEGS.

ROMAN: Er, no thanks, Gita. I'll just have the facial today.

BUBBLES STARTS MASSAGING HIS THIGHS AND WORKS UPWARDS.

ROMAN: That's... very intimate.

Ooh that's good, that's ample. Do I have to pay extra for this?

EPISODE ELEVEN

BUBBLES: (ATTEMPTING JAPANESE ACCENT) Do you like?

ROMAN: Ooh... very pleasurable.

BUBBLES SLIPS OFF HER ROBE. SHE GUIDES ROMAN'S HAND TO HER BREAST.

ROMAN: Ooh that's good, that's ample. Do I have to pay extra for this?

BUBBLES: (ATTEMPTING JAPANESE ACCENT) No, no, it's all part of the service...

BUBBLES CLIMBS ON TOP OF ROMAN.

ROMAN: Ooh, you're bigger than you look, Gita.

BUBBLES: (USING OWN VOICE) You always liked me on top, didn't you, darling?

ROMAN SHAKES OFF THE CUCUMBER AND SEES HIS EX-WIFE ON TOP OF HIM.

ROMAN: Yeah... oh... Bubbles!

BUBBLES: (STILL HUMPING) Hello, darling.

ROMAN: Bubbles, you gotta stop... Quite soon.

ENTER DESIREE.

DESIREE: Baby! What are you doing, baby?!

BUBBLES: Hello, darling.

ROMAN: It's not what it looks like.

DESIREE: Get off him, you jezebel!

BUBBLES: Don't worry. I'm going.

BUBBLES MANAGES TO CLIMB DOWN AND HEADS FOR THE DOOR. AS SHE GETS THERE, SHE TURNS.

BUBBLES: Hope I haven't spoiled your honeymoony, darlings.

BUBBLES EXITS, LAUGHING. DESIREE TURNS ON ROMAN, WHO IS NOW SAT ON THE SIDE OF THE BED.

DESIREE: How could you do this to me, baby? With your ex-wife!

ROMAN: I was tricked into it. I'm completely innocent.

DESIREE: Is that what you want? You want to get back with that harlot?

ROMAN: No, no. Honestly. I hated every minute of it.

ROMAN GETS UP. WE SEE, THROUGH HIS TOWEL, THAT HE IS VERY ERECT.

DESIREE: (CLOCKING HIS ERECTION) Nim-nim-nim-nim-nim-nim-nim-nim! (SLAPPING IT) Naughty!

SHE GRABS IT AND LEADS HIM OUT.

ORVILLE – WHERE'S KEITH?

INT: SUPERMARKET.

TOM V/O: Our next stop on our journey is this supermarket, situated in the ancient Roman city of Breakdance 2: Electric Boogaloo.

WE SEE A LARGE GREEN DUCK WEARING A NAPPY FROM BEHIND. HE'S LOOKING AT THE CRISPS. A MAN APPROACHES.

MAN: Excuse me?

THE DUCK TURNS ROUND. WE SEE THAT IT IS ORVILLE THE DUCK OF KEITH HARRIS AND ORVILLE FAME. HE SPEAKS IN A NORMAL VOICE.

ORVILLE: Yeah?

MAN: Are you Orville?

ORVILLE: Yeah.

MAN: Can I have your autograph please?

ORVILLE: Er yeah. Have you got a pen?

THE MAN GIVES HIM A PEN AND SOME PAPER.

ORVILLE: Sorry. Who's it to?

MAN: It's me. John.

MAN: (CHUCKLING) So where's Keith Harris then?

ORVILLE: I don't know.

MAN: It would just be funny if he was here.

ORVILLE: Yeah, it's work. We don't spend every minute of the day together. We do have our own lives as well.

MAN: He's very funny.

ORVILLE: (WEARY) Yeah, yeah. He's a really funny guy.

> I'm actually going up for a part in *The Bill* next week.

ORVILLE GIVES THE MAN BACK THE SIGNED PIECE OF PAPER.

MAN: Are you working on anything together at the moment?

ORVILLE: No, we're sort of having a sabbatical at the moment. I'm trying to concentrate on some straight acting. I'm actually going up for a part in *The Bill* next week.

MAN: Oh right.

ORVILLE: Yeah, it's a one-off. It's the part of a racist copper.

MAN: Oh good luck with that. Sorry before I go. I know you must get this all the time. Could you just do Keith's voice for me?

ORVILLE: (SIGHS) Look, I'm just out shopping today. I don't really wanna sort of draw attention to myself...

MAN: Sorry, I'll let you get on.

ORVILLE: Okay.

THE MAN GOES. ANOTHER MAN APPEARS, GRINNING.

MAN 2: Oi Orville, where's Keith?

ORVILLE SIGHS.

ORVILLE: (MUTTERS TO HIMSELF) Oh for god's sake.

CURRY 2 – CHICKEN JALFREZI

INT: SUBURBAN INDIAN RESTAURANT. PAT AND HER HUSBAND DON ARE PERUSING THE MENU. A WAITER STANDS BY.

TOM V/O: At this restaurant in Upper Gonad, couple Pat and Don are ordering a meal.

PAT: ...and an onion bhaji, please. That is quite mild, isn't it?

WAITER: Yes. And for sir?

DON: I'll just have a plate of curry powder, please?

PAT: Don, no!

DON: Alright. I'll have the chicken jalfrezi. But can you have it spicy, please? I do like it spicy.

THE WAITER NODS AND EXITS.

PAT: Service is slow today.

DON: Yeah, I'm not coming here again.

THE WAITER APPEARS IMMEDIATELY WITH THE FOOD.

DON: Oh, here he is.

PAT: About time.

WAITER: Sorry for the delay.

THE WAITER PUTS THE FOOD DOWN. PAT HAS A TASTE.

PAT: Hmm, mine's lovely. How's yours?

DON TAKES A BITE.

Hmmm. Ooooh - Godzilla dum dum de dum Godzilla dum dum de dum Godzilla dum dum de dum and Godzooki. The fallen Madonna with big boobies! Monkey! Runaround, now! Mr Spencer! Very flat - Norfolk.

What do you take me for - a fool? Ladies and gentlemen, Miss Barbara Dixon. Wooooah Bodyform! Bodyform for comfort, Bodyform for confidence, Bodyform for you!

DON: Hmmm. (PULLS A FACE) Ooooh - Godzilla dum dum de dum Godzilla dum dum de dum Godzilla dum dum de dum and Godzooki. The fallen Madonna with big boobies! Monkey! Runaround, now! Mr Spencer! Very flat - Norfolk. What do you take me for - a fool? (PUTS ON A PAIR OF GLASSES) Ladies and gentlemen, Miss Barbara Dixon. (TAKES THEM OFF AGAIN) Wooooah Bodyform! Bodyform for comfort, Bodyform for confidence, Bodyform for you!

DON DRINKS A SIP OF WATER.

DON: Not too spicy at all. Woooh Macarena!

SEBASTIAN AND MICHAEL — AFFAIR

EXT: NO 10 DOWNING STREET. A POLICEMAN STANDS GUARD. SEBASTIAN ARRIVES AND, AS HE ENTERS NUMBER 10, TILTS THE POLICEMAN'S HELMET AND CROOKS HIS ARM TO MAKE HIS APPEAR CAMP.

TOM V/O: The current Prime Minister, Michael Stevens, is proving very popular in the polls. Almost as popular as our previous leader, General Udu Umbego.

INT: PM'S OFFICE. MICHAEL IS WITH HIS WIFE, SARAH, WHO IS HOLDING THE LATEST EDITION OF THE SUN. THE HEADLINE READS "MY LOVE AFFAIR WITH PM".

SARAH: It's just so humiliating for me.

MICHAEL: I know, darling. I'm so sorry.

SARAH: Well, I suppose it was going to come out, sooner or later.

MICHAEL: Look, tomorrow it'll just be old news.

SARAH: Let's put out a statement through the Press Secretary saying it's a private matter.

MICHAEL: Sarah, we're gonna get through this together.

THEY KISS EACH OTHER AND HAVE A LONG, CLOSE HUG. ENTER SEBASTIAN.

SEBASTIAN: Morning, Prime Minister.

MICHAEL: Hi, Sebastian. We're just a little upset here.

MICHAEL AND SARAH CONTINUE TO HUG. SEBASTIAN LURKS. HE EDGES TOWARDS THE COUPLE AND EVENTUALLY JOINS IN THE HUG. SEBASTIAN AND SARAH STARE AT EACH OTHER.

I mean, as if you'd have an affair with the old Education Secretary. Look at her. She's a right dog.

This book's going to give me a rough ride...

SEBASTIAN: Your car's here.

SARAH BREAKS IT OFF.

SARAH: I'd better dash. I'm due in court.

MICHAEL: Good luck, darling.

SARAH EXITS. SEBASTIAN CONTINUES TO HUG MICHAEL.

MICHAEL: (PULLING AWAY) So Sebastian, I suppose you've heard the news.

SEBASTIAN: Yeah, and I bought the book. I mean, as if you'd have an affair with the old Education Secretary. Look at her. She's a right dog.

SEBASTIAN HOLDS UP A GLOSSY HARDBACK BOOK. IT'S CALLED *DIVISION BELL* BY ANGELA BELL MP.

MICHAEL: Sebastian –

SEBASTIAN: (READING FROM THE BOOK) Oh, this is my favourite bit: 'Michael gazed at me from across the room at the party conference. Twenty minutes later, our bodies were united in passionate political union.' Ha ha! Lying cow!

MICHAEL: It's true. We were both young MPs, both far away from home. Sarah and I had had our problems and one thing led to another.

SEBASTIAN: (DEEP VOICE) What?

MICHAEL: It finished a long time ago. Sarah's known about it for years. We've accepted it and moved on.

SEBASTIAN: And just when do you think you were going to tell me?

MICHAEL: Sebastian, quite honestly it's none of your business.

SEBASTIAN: You're still seeing her.

MICHAEL: Don't be silly.

SEBASTIAN: I can smell her! You wait until I'm gone and then you have her, you have her on this couch! Like this, is it?

SEBASTIAN IS ON ALL FOURS ON THE SOFA.

SEBASTIAN: 'Ooh give it to me'? Or is it like this?

SEBASTIAN LIES ON HIS BACK WITH HIS LEGS IN THE AIR.

SEBASTIAN: 'Ooh that's deep.'

SEBASTIAN GETS UP.

SEBASTIAN: Do you laugh about me when you're together? Do you? HA HA HA!

MICHAEL: It finished fifteen years ago.

SEBASTIAN: Prove it. Have her killed. You're the Prime Minister, one call will do it! It's the only way I'll know she means nothing to you!

SEBASTIAN HOLDS THE PHONE TO MICHAEL'S EAR.

SECRETARY: (ON PHONE) MI5, Sue speaking?

MICHAEL: I'm so sorry, I've got the wrong number.

SUE: (ON PHONE) No bother, goodbye.

MICHAEL TAKES THE PHONE AND PUTS IT DOWN.

MICHAEL: Come now, Sebastian –

SEBASTIAN: (TEARFUL) Just tell me why? What did I do wrong? What does she give you that I can't?

MICHAEL: Look! This book's going to give me a rough ride for the next week and I need people around me who can help me through it. Now, if you can't I'll find someone else who can. Okay?

SEBASTIAN: Yeah, fine.

Hi. Slut's over there.

A BUZZER SOUNDS.

SECRETARY: (ON INTERCOM) The German Chancellor is here.

MICHAEL: Thank you. Would you like to show him in, Sebastian?

SEBASTIAN WALKS TO THE DOOR AND LETS IN THE GERMAN CHANCELLOR.

SEBASTIAN: Hi. Slut's over there.

SEBASTIAN EXITS TRIUMPHANTLY, LEAVING A SHOCKED-LOOKING CHANCELLOR.

ALAN/DONKEY HOSPICE

EXT: CITY CENTRE.

TOM V/O: Our next stop is the southern town of Achingballs...

A KIND-LOOKING MAN (ALAN) IS HOLDING A CHARITY COLLECTION TIN AND WEARING A SASH. BOTH READ 'DONKEY HOSPICE'. HE CARRIES A ROLL OF STICKERS AND CALLS OUT SOFTLY TO PASSERS-BY.

ALAN: Donkey hospice? Money for the donkey hospice?

There's some
stickers for you.

AN ELDERLY COUPLE STOP AND DIG OUT SOME MONEY. THEY PUT IT IN THE TIN.

ALAN: Thank you.

LADY: My father had a donkey.

ALAN: Oh did he? (LAUGHS) There's some stickers for you.

ALAN PUTS A STICKER ON EACH OF THE OLD LADY'S BREASTS.

ALAN: And there's one for you.

HE PUTS A STICKER ON THE OLD MAN'S GENITAL REGION.

ALAN: The donkeys will be very pleased. Thank you.

THE BEMUSED COUPLE LEAVE, SLIGHTLY UNSURE AS TO WHETHER THAT JUST HAPPENED.

ALAN: Donkey hospice?

MAGGIE AND JUDY — JAMES

TOM V/O: In the village of Pox, Maggie is delivering the parish newsletter.

EXT: VILLAGE LANE/JUDY'S COTTAGE. MAGGIE IS WALKING ALONG CHIRPILY, CARRYING A SHEAF OF PARISH NEWSLETTERS. SHE ARRIVES AT THE FRONT DOOR OF A SMALL COTTAGE AND RINGS THE BELL. JUDY ANSWERS.

JUDY: Hello, Maggie.

MAGGIE: Hello, Judy. I've got the new parish newsletter for you.

JUDY: Thank you very much. I would ask you in but I'm a little busy at the moment. My daughter's here with her fiancé.

MAGGIE: Oh, well I'd love to meet him.

JUDY: I'm not sure that's a good idea...

MAGGIE: He sounds so wonderful. You told me he went to Cambridge and he's now a barrister.

JUDY: Yes, um, well, come in then.

MAGGIE FOLLOWS JUDY IN. THE PAIR WALK INTO THE DRAWING ROOM.

JUDY: We're just in the drawing room.

INT. LOVELY OLD-FASHIONED ROOM, WITH A PARROT IN A CAGE IN THE CORNER. MAGGIE SPOTS JUDY'S DAUGHTER, OLIVIA, AND HER FIANCÉ JAMES, A HANDSOME BLACK MAN.

MAGGIE: Wooooooooah!

MAGGIE LOOKS HORRIFIED. JUDY SENSES WHAT IS HAPPENING AND TRIES TO PAPER OVER THE CRACKS.

JUDY: Um, Olivia you know.

MAGGIE NODS AND GRUNTS.

OLIVIA: Hello.

PARROT: (MIMICS) Hello.

JAMES: Pleased to meet you. I'm James.

MAGGIE: (OVERLY ENTHUSIASTIC) Yes, lovely to meet you.

SHE SHAKES HIS HAND LIMPLY AND THEN WIPES IT ON HER CARDIGAN.

OLIVIA: Did Mummy tell you, we're getting married in August?

MAGGIE: Well, I really must deliver these he's black newsletters so...

JAMES: Do stay for a cup of tea.

OLIVIA: And you must have one of these. They're delicious.

JUDY PROFFERS A PLATE OF CAKE SLICES TO MAGGIE, WHO TAKES ONE AND HAS A BITE.

MAGGIE: Oh, thank you. (TO OLIVIA) Your mother's fruit cake is legendary.

JAMES: Actually, my mother made it. Let me get you some tea.

Maggie! Please! I've just had the carpet shampooed!

JAMES EXITS THE ROOM. MAGGIE STARTS TO GROAN, AS IF SHE IS ABOUT TO BE SICK. JUDY AND OLIVIA SHARE A LOOK OF CONCERN.

OLIVIA: Are you alright?

JUDY: Oh no, Maggie! Please! I've just had the carpet shampooed!

MAGGIE NODS AND THEN SPEWS ALL OVER OLIVIA. MAGGIE IS THEN SICK ALL OVER JUDY BEFORE PUKING OVER THE PARROT. THE SCENE IS ONE OF SILENT DEVASTATION. JAMES ENTERS CARRYING A TRAY, WITH A TEAPOT AND FOUR TEACUPS. IT TAKES HIM A SECOND TO NOTICE WHAT HAS JUST HAPPENED.

JAMES: Now do you take... (SHOCKED) Sugar?

MAGGIE: Actually, I really must deliver these.

MAGGIE HOLDS UP A PILE OF NEWSLETTERS, COVERED IN SICK.

MAGGIE: (TO JAMES) Lovely to have met you. (TO OLIVIA AND JUDY) Goodbye. Goodbye.

SHE EXITS, PASSING JAMES ON THE WAY OUT OF THE ROOM.

PARROT: (HAPPILY) Goodbye.

LOU AND ANDY — SPEEDING

INT: LOU'S VAN.

TOM V/O: Meanwhile, Lou has pawned his shoes to take Andy on a day trip.

LOU: Did you enjoy our little trip to Legoland?

ANDY: Nah, it was all just Lego.

LOU: Oh. Well, I'm sorry. I did say.

ANDY: (SUDDENLY TURNING TO LOU) What time is it?

LOU: Four-thirty.

ANDY: We're gonna miss *Dogtanian And The Three Muskehounds*!

LOU: Well there's not a lot I can do. I don't want to break the speed limit.

ANDY: Faster.

LOU: But I thought you didn't like *Dogtanian And The Three Muskehounds*. I thought you said that the Dumas' classic characters into their canine counterparts was decidedly lacklustre.

ANDY: Yeah, I know.

LOU: I promise I'll get you home in time for *Jossy's Giants*.

ANDY: Dogtanian.

LOU: (SIGHS) Oh dear.

HE CHECKS HIS WING MIRROR AND SPEEDS UP.

ANDY: Faster, faster.

LOU: I'm going faster. I'm doing eighty!

BEHIND THEM A POLICE SIREN IS HEARD.

LOU: Oh no. It's PC Plod. Oh no.

THE MOTORBIKE PULLS ALONGSIDE AND THE POLICEMAN INDICATES TO
LOU TO PULL IN.

LOU: Yes, I will pull over, sir. Yes.

BOTH VEHICLES STOP.

LOU: Oh, he doesn't look happy. He's got a right cob on.

EXT: ROAD. LOU HAS PULLED OVER. THE POLICEMAN ON A MOTORBIKE HAS
PARKED UP AND IS APPROACHING.

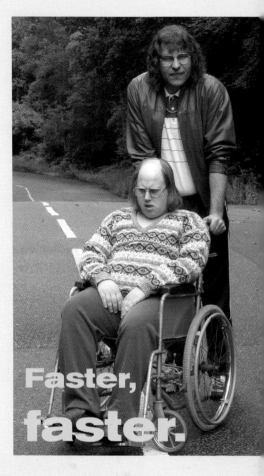

Faster, faster.

POLICEMAN: (TAPPING ON THE WINDOW) Step out of the vehicle
please, sir.

LOU: I'm very sorry, Mr Policeman sir.

POLICEMAN: Right, I'd like your full name, please.

AS THIS CONVERSATION TAKES PLACE, ANDY EXITS THE VEHICLE UNNOTICED, SCAMPERS ROUND AND GETS ON THE
MOTORBIKE.

LOU: It's Louis Bob Todd.

POLICEMAN: Have you any idea how fast you were driving, sir?

LOU: I'm very sorry, Mr Policeman. I've got a friend here who's in a wheelchair who's
very keen to get back...

THE REST OF THEIR CONVERSATION IS DROWNED OUT BY THE REVVING OF THE MOTORBIKE AS ANDY RIDES AWAY. HE
DOES A WHEELIE AND ACCELERATES WILDLY INTO THE DISTANCE, BURNING RUBBER.

TOM V/O: And tonight's episode of Little Britain was shown as a tribute to Matt Lucas
and David Walliams, who are sadly still with us. Our thoughts are with their friends
and family at this difficult time. Goodbye.

THE ADVENTURES OF LOU & ANDY

Lou and Andy are off to a judo lesson. Judo was invented in 1956 by a Hampshire housewife Kathy Judo.

OOH THAT'S GOOD BECAUSE I'VE NEVER DONE JUDO BEFORE

YEAH I KNOW

EVERYBODY FIND A PARTNER

LOU YOU CAN GO WITH YUKO

WHAT A KERFUFFLE!

LET ME JUST TAKE OFF MY GLASSES

EPISODE *four*

TOM V/O: Britain, Britain, Britain. For centuries now, Britishers have shaped the world. Mahatma Ghandi, Leonardo Da Vinci, Ludwig van Beethoven, all British. Even Jesus Christ was from Woking in Surrey. But what of the ordinary people folk what sort of live here and that? Let's meet them. Watch us wreck the mike, watch us wreck the mike, watch us wreck the mike. Psyche!

MRS EMERY — LIBRARY

TOM V/O: In Britain, if an old person reaches a hundred, they receive a telegram from the Queen. If they reach two hundred her majesty comes round to their house and personally gives them a bikini wax.

INT: LIBRARY. MRS EMERY IS BROWSING THE AISLES. SHE BUMPS INTO A YOUNG MOTHER (KAREN) WHOSE BABY IS IN A BUGGY.

KAREN: Hello, Mrs Emery?

MRS EMERY: Oh hallo, dear. Ooh, hasn't he grown?

KAREN: Yeah, he's eighteen months now.

MRS EMERY: Oh he's lovely! You still working down the cafe?

KAREN: No, I had to give that up but I'll be able to go back if I can get him into a nursery.

AT THIS POINT, WITHOUT BATTING AN EYELID, MRS EMERY STARTS PEEING COPIOUS AMOUNTS.

MRS EMERY: Oh, is there a good one near here?

KAREN: (SHOCKED) Um. I think so.

MRS EMERY: My friend Joan. Her youngest granddaughter goes to a very good one up by the baths. Do you know that one?

KAREN: Yeah.

MRS EMERY: I think there's a long waiting list. Is he on the waiting list?

KAREN: No. He's not.

KAREN: Right, well. Nice to see you again, Mrs Emery.

SHE STARTS TO BACK OFF DURING THE ABOVE.

MRS EMERY: Yes, dear. Oh hang on a sec. Would he like a jelly baby?

KAREN: Um. No, I don't really like him having sweets.

MRS EMERY: Go on. One won't hurt. There you go.

SHE POPS A SWEET INTO THE BABY'S MOUTH.

KAREN: What do you say?

THE BABY DOESN'T RESPOND.

MRS EMERY: Oh, he's gone all shy. I'll see you later, dear.

MRS EMERY GOES TO LEAVE.

MRS EMERY: Oh, mind that. There must be a leak here or something. Ta ta.

AS SHE WANDERS OFF. WE STAY ON A SHOCKED-LOOKING KAREN.

There must be a leak

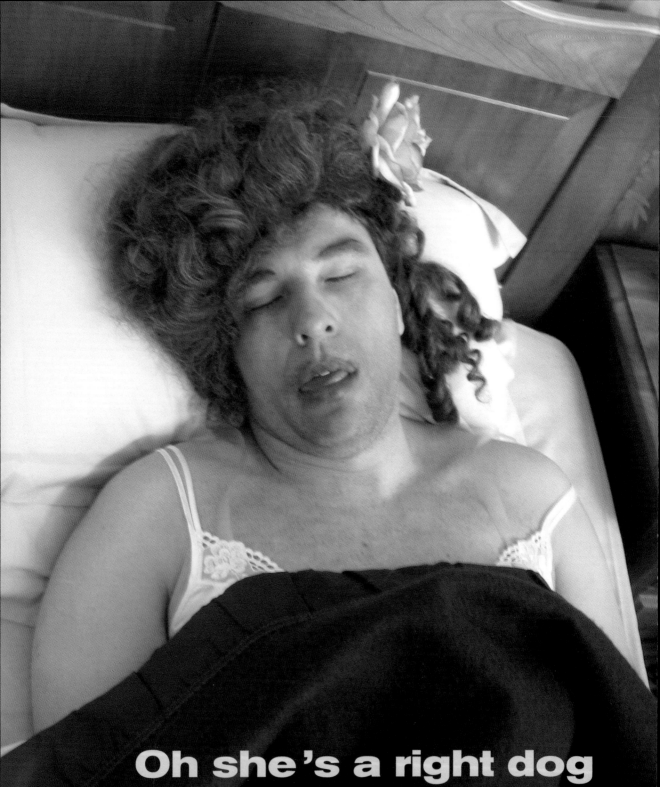

Oh she's a right dog

EMILY AND FLORENCE — HEN NIGHT

EXT: SEA FRONT.

TOM V/O: Transvestism was invented in 1986 by Dr Neil Transvestite, who came upon the idea purely by chance, when he was investigating nuclear fission theory whilst wearing his wife's nightie.

EMILY AND FLORENCE ARE CYCLING ALONG ON THEIR TANDEM, CALLING OUT TO PASSERS-BY.

INT: BAR. EMILY AND FLORENCE ENTER. A FEW HEADS TURN. THEY HEAD FOR THE BAR.

EMILY: Two ladies, out on a hen night.

FLORENCE: Pay no heed!

EMILY: (LOUDLY) Good evening, barman.

BARMAN: Yes gentlemen?

EMILY: Two sweet sherries, s'il-vous plait.

FLORENCE: With lager chasers.

EMILY THROWS FLORENCE A LOOK. THE BEMUSED BARMAN GETS THE DRINKS.

FLORENCE: Well, my dear Emily, it is to be your final night as a single lady.

EMILY: That's right, Florence, my lady friend. I'm getting married in the morning. To a man.

FLORENCE: Well you would be, being a lady.

EMILY: So I suppose if any man should wish to take advantage of me on my one final night of freedom they should (RAISING VOLUME) speak up now.

THERE IS SILENCE. EVERYBODY IN THE PUB FREEZES. EMILY LOOKS SUITABLY EMBARRASSED. ONE OF THE CUSTOMERS DROPS A PIN. WE HEAR IT.

FLORENCE: Well, it's still early.

THE BARMAN GIVES EMILY AND FLORENCE THEIR DRINKS.

BARMAN: There you are. There is a gay bar down the road, you know. That's where most of the trannies go.

EMILY: Well, thank you for warning us, barman. We don't want to go there, do we?

FLORENCE: Ooh no, ha ha.

SUDDENLY FIVE BOISTEROUS, DRUNK GEORDIE LADS IN THEIR EARLY TWENTIES AND OUT ON A STAG NIGHT PILE IN AND HEAD FOR THE BAR.

EPISODE

GROUP: (CHANT) 'Get yer tits out, get yer tits out for the lads.'

ONE PARTICULARLY INEBRIATED MEMBER – KEITH – HAS LIPSTICK KISSES ON HIS CHEEKS AND AN 'L' PLATE STUCK TO HIM. HIS BEST MAN – TOMMY – CLICKS HIS FINGERS.

TOMMY: 'Ere, barman. Our mate here is getting married on Saturday. We want six double vodka and Red Bulls'.

BARMAN: (ACKNOWLEDGING ORDER) Alright, lads.

THE BARMAN GOES TO GET THE GROUP'S ORDER. FLORENCE EYES THE LADS AND SCREWS UP HER NOSE.

FLORENCE: Ugh. Look at them. They're so drunk, they don't know what they're doing.

EMILY: (WITH A GLINT IN HER EYE) Yes.

EMILY WAVES COYLY AT THE LADS.

INT: HOTEL BATHROOM/BEDROOM. KEITH IS URINATING. TOMMY WALKS IN AND STARES AT HIMSELF IN THE MIRROR. HE GRABS SOME ALKA-SELTZER. THEY BOTH LOOK ROUGH.

TOMMY: Oh man, how much did we drink last night?

KEITH: Dunno. I was bladdered.

TOMMY: Have you seen what I came back with?

Morning!

THEY OPEN THE BATHROOM DOOR AND TAKE A PEAK. WE SEE EMILY LYING IN BED, SNORING HEAVILY. HER WIG IS
ASKEW AND HER MAKE-UP HAS SMEARED. SHE HAS STUBBLE. KEITH LAUGHS.

KEITH: (SOTTO) Oh she's a right dog.

TOMMY: Well, you can talk.

TOMMY INDICATES TOWARDS KEITH'S BED, WHERE FLORENCE IS SITTING UP, CHEERILY SMOKING A PIPE AND
READING *THE TIMES*.

FLORENCE: (MAN'S VOICE) Morning.

EPISODE

DUDLEY AND TING TONG — FAMILY

EXT: ROAD/DUDLEY'S FLAT IN BACKGROUND

TOM V/O: It's a crisp October morning in Bruise and Dudley has nipped out for a newspaper.

DUDLEY, WITH A COPY OF *SPORTING LIFE*, APPROACHES THE ENTRANCE TO HIS FLATS. ATTACHED TO THE FENCE IS AN OFFICIAL-LOOKING POLICE FATAL ACCIDENT NOTICE AND SOME WITHERED-LOOKING BOUQUETS OF FLOWERS. WITHOUT STOPPING, HE TAKES ONE OF THE BUNCHES OF FLOWERS.

INT: DUDLEY'S FLAT/HALL. WE HEAR A WOMAN'S VOICE AND A CUPBOARD CLOSING. DUDLEY ENTERS THE FLAT.

DUDLEY: Ting Tong?

TING TONG: Oh, hello Mr Dudley.

DUDLEY: I bought you some flowers.

TING TONG TAKES THE FLOWERS.

TING TONG: Oh, you so thoughtful.

THEY KISS AFFECTIONATELY.

DUDLEY: Were you... talking to somebody?

TING TONG: No, Mr Dudley. No. I was just making you traditional Thai breakfast.

WE SEE THAT TING TONG IS FRYING SOMETHING THAT LOOKS LIKE A PAIR OF TESTICLES. DUDLEY WINCES.

DUDLEY: Ah, oh. I think I'm gonna need some HP sauce on that.

DUDLEY OPENS A CUPBOARD. INSIDE ARE A NUMBER OF CONDIMENTS AND BELOW THEM, AN OLD THAI LADY, DEADPAN. DUDLEY TAKES THE HP SAUCE.

DUDLEY: Hullo.

DUDLEY CLOSES THE CUPBOARD. HE OPENS IT AND HAS ANOTHER LOOK. HE CLOSES IT AGAIN.

DUDLEY: Ting Tong?

TING TONG: Yes, Mr Dudley?

DUDLEY: (FLATLY) There's an elderly Thai lady in the cupboard.

TING TONG: Is there, Mr Dudley?

There's an elderly Thai lady in the cupboard

She says she very look forward to come live with us

DUDLEY: Yes. Yes, there is.

TING TONG: Oh yeah, I was gonna tell you. Yeah. Yeah. That is just my mother, she is come to stay for a little bit.

TING TONG OPENS THE CUPBOARD.

TING TONG: Mother, this Mr Dudley, I was telling you about.

THE MOTHER GETS OUT OF THE CUPBOARD AND NODS POLITELY AT DUDLEY, BEFORE SPEAKING TO HIM IN THAI.

DUDLEY: Yes. (TO TING TONG) What's she saying?

TING TONG: Oh. She says she very look forward to come live with us.

DUDLEY: (TO MOTHER) Excuse us.

DUDLEY TAKES TING TONG TO ONE SIDE.

DUDLEY: Ting Tong, we can't be having your mother living here. It's not gonna work.

TING TONG: It would only be for a few year. Anyway, she be dead soon.

DUDLEY: No. (TO MOTHER) I'm sorry, Mrs Macadangdang. You're gonna have to go.

MOTHER PLEADS IN THAI, AT LENGTH.

TING TONG: You heard what she said.

DUDLEY: I don't care what she said. She's gonna have to go!

TING TONG AND MOTHER CRY AND KNEEL AT DUDLEY'S FEET. THEY CLING TO HIM EITHER SIDE.

DUDLEY: No, I'm sorry – I said no!

TING TONG: But we'll do anything if you let her stay. Anything.

DUDLEY LOOKS AT THE TWO WOMEN CLINGING ONTO HIM.

DUDLEY: Anything?

TING TONG: Anything.

DUDLEY: Well. Maybe she could stay with us tonight, at least. (TO TING TONG) You... er... got any sisters?

BUBBLES DEVERE — SAUNA

EXT: HILL GRANGE HEALTH SPA

TOM V/O: At Hill Grange Health Spa one-time body double for Joan Collins, Bubbles DeVere, is on her way to the sauna.

BUBBLES PASSES GITA

GITA: Hello, Miss Bubble.

BUBBLES: Don't forget I have a mashed potato foot massage at four, darling.

INT: HILL GRANGE HEALTH SPA/SAUNA. ROMAN IS ALONE ON THE LOWER BENCH IN THE SAUNA. HE IS READING 'PLUMPERS'. A NAKED BUBBLES ENTERS. ROMAN QUICKLY HIDES THE MAGAZINE.

I need to ask you a question, darling...

BUBBLES: Hello, darling.

ROMAN: Oh hello.

BUBBLES: I'm quite naked. Do you see?

ROMAN: Yeah, I do see that, yeah.

BUBBLES COMES AND SITS DOWN NEXT TO ROMAN.

BUBBLES: I need to ask you a question, darling.

ROMAN: What is it?

BUBBLES: Why did you leave me, darling? Why?

ROMAN: Well you know, I always found you very attractive, but I preferred you before you lost all that weight.

BUBBLES: I know. I'm like a stick now.

ROMAN: And then Desiree come along and – well, I'm sorry, Bubbles but there is so *much* of her to love.

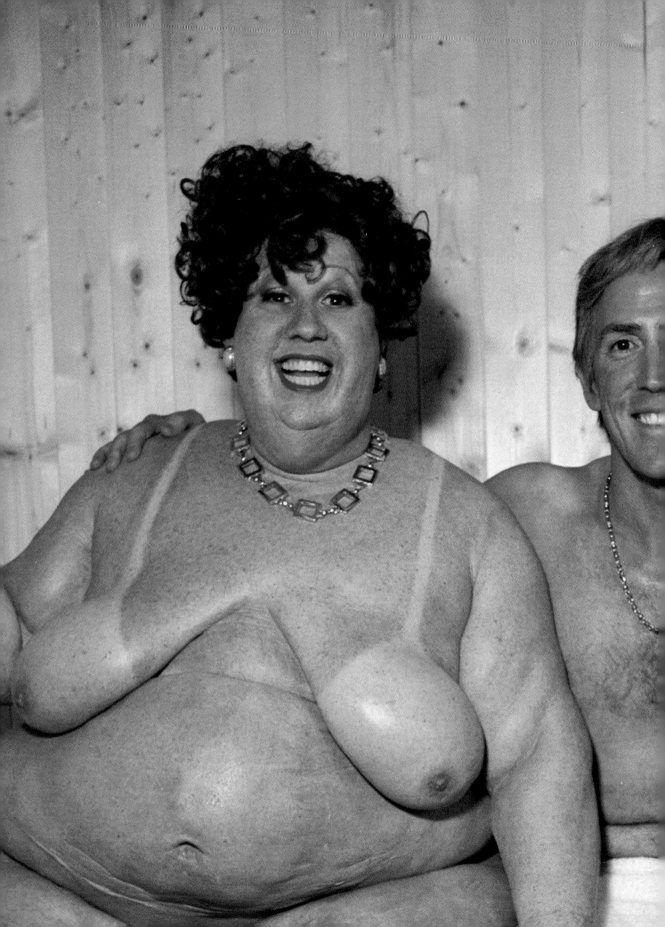

BUBBLES: But Roman.

ROMAN: (SUCCUMBING) Oh Bubbles.

THE DOOR OPENS. DESIREE ENTERS. SHE IS NAKED AND NOTICEABLY A LOT BIGGER THAN BUBBLES.

DESIREE: Hnm-nm-nm-nm-nm-nm- Hello, babies.

BUBBLES GROWLS

DESIREE: Not interrupting anything, am I?

ROMAN: No. We was just talking about old times.

DESIREE: (TO BUBBLES) I'll give you old times.

DESIREE LOOKS SUSPICIOUSLY AT BUBBLES. SHE PLONKS HERSELF DOWN ON THE OTHER SIDE OF ROMAN THEN MAKES A BIG DISPLAY OF COSYING UP TO HIM.

DESIREE: So, are you looking forward to our synchronised foot massage later?

ROMAN: Oh, yes I am.

DESIREE: I hear it is very aphrodisiacy.

AN EXCITED ROMAN STARTS TO FONDLE DESIREE. BUBBLES BRISTLES. SHE RISES AND HEADS FOR THE DOOR.

BUBBLES: I'll be back, darlings!

DESIREE: (TRIUMPHANT) Bye bye baby!

BUBBLES EXITS, SLAMMING THE DOOR.

BUBBLES: (TO HERSELF) Must get bigger. Must get bigger.

INT: SUPERMARKET. A NAKED BUBBLES APPEARS WITH HER TROLLEY LADEN WITH LOTS OF HIGH-FAT FOODS. OTHER SHOPPERS LOOK AT HER SHOCKED. ONE PARTICULAR WOMAN LOOKS FOR A SHORT WHILE. BUBBLES SNAPS AT HER.

BUBBLES: Why don't you take a photo? It'll last longer!

I'm quite naked. Do you see?

Lunch alright?

DEATHBED

INT: HOSPITAL WARD.

TOM V/O: (SOMBRE) It's a sad day at St Shaznay's hospital as this old man is nearing the end.

SCREENS SHIELD A TEARFUL FAMILY (TWO BROTHERS AND THEIR WIVES), SITTING ROUND THE BED OF A VERY OLD MAN (WARREN), WHO APPEARS TO BE DYING. A NURSE IS WITH THEM. THE MOOD IS ONE OF PEACE AND CALM. ONE OF THE COUPLES HOLD HANDS.

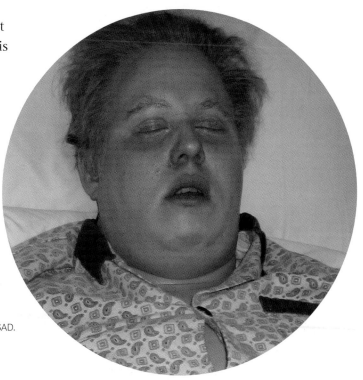

WARREN: (STRAINED) ...And I don't want you to be sad for me. I've had a wonderful life and I love you all very very much... Goodbye.

WARREN CLOSES HIS EYES. THE FAMILY LOOK SAD.

BROTHER 1: (TO NURSE) Has he gone?

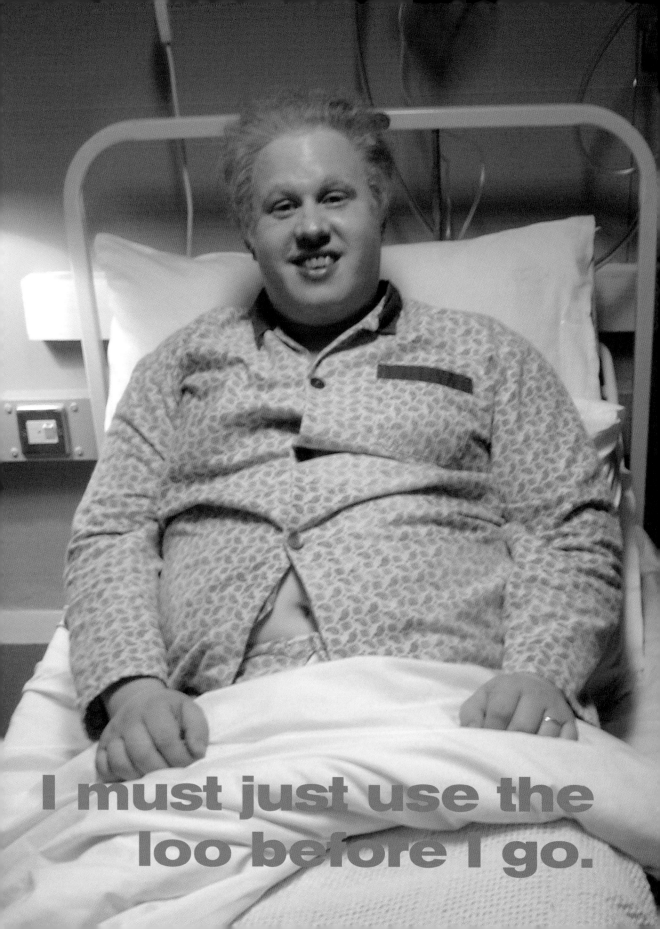

I must just use the
loo before I go.

Well... this is... goodbye.

WARREN: (EYES CLOSED) Not just yet.

WARREN OPENS HIS EYES.

WARREN: How's everybody else?

ALL: Fine thank you.

BROTHER 2: Mustn't grumble.

WARREN: Lunch alright?

ALL: Fine.

WARREN: Well... this is... goodbye.

WARREN CLOSES HIS EYES. BEAT. WIFE 2 STARTS TO CRY...

WARREN: ...Any minute now.

PAUSE. WARREN BREATHES UNEASILY.

WARREN: (QUIETLY) Well, may I say how wonderful it is to have my family around me at the very very end. Goodbye.

WARREN CLOSES HIS EYES. PAUSE. THAT APPEARS TO BE THE END. THE FAMILY MOP AWAY TEARS.

WARREN: I must just use the loo before I go.

WARREN GETS UP QUITE ABLY AND EXITS.

CAROL – CAPTAIN CORELLI

EXT: 'SUNSEACHERS' TRAVEL AGENTS. WE SEE CAROL BEER INSIDE
THE SHOP, STANDING AT THE WINDOW. SHE PINS UP A POSTER THAT
READS 'SIBERIA – CAMPING HOLIDAY – £219'.

TOM V/O: The first travel agents in Britain opened
in 1976. Prior to that, people would stay at home
and give themselves food poisoning.

INT: TRAVEL AGENTS. CAROL BEER IS SAT AT HER DESK. AN IRISH
PRIEST IN A DOG COLLAR SITS OPPOSITE HER.

PRIEST: ...And you've nothing at all going to Lourdes?

CAROL TYPES.

CAROL: Computer says no.

PRIEST: Oh, what a shame.

CAROL: It says it's all pilgrimmed out. If you like
religion I can do you a fly-drive to Mecca?

PRIEST: No. I think I'll leave it, thank you.

THE PRIEST GOES TO LEAVE. CAROL COUGHS INTO HIS FACE. AS HE
EXITS, A LADY IN HER FORTIES (ANITA) ENTERS AND SITS OPPOSITE
HER.

ANITA: Hello.

CAROL: I've been sat down all day. Do you mind if I
just stretch my legs?

ANITA: Of course.

CAROL RISES AND, WITH A BLANK FACE, DOES A FANTASTICALLY
ENERGETIC ARRAY OF EXERCISES. SHE THEN SITS BACK DOWN
AGAIN, DEADPAN.

CAROL: Right.

ANITA: Um. I was watching this film last night –
Captain Corelli's Mandolin – and I was really wanting
to visit the island of Kefalonia, where they filmed it.

CAROL TYPES.

CAROL: Computer says no.

ANITA: Oh.

CAROL: If you're a film fan I can take you to where they filmed *Midnight Express*.

ANITA: No. No, thank you.

CAROL: I've got some rooms in *The Towering Inferno*.

ANITA: No.

CAROL: I've got a lovely cruise on the ship where they filmed *The Poseidon Adventure*.

ANITA: I don't think so.

CAROL: No, it's not for everybody. It is upside down. I've got a two-for-one deal on a canoeing trip where they filmed *Deliverance*.

ANITA: No, thank you.

CAROL: It says here the locals are very friendly.

ANITA: Look, I really only do want to go to Kefalonia.

CAROL: Oh, wasn't some of *Captain Corelli* filmed in Centerparcs? I can get you a very good deal there.

ANITA: No. Look, I'm just gonna leave it.

ANITA RISES AND HEADS FOR THE DOOR.

CAROL: And was none of it filmed on a Club 18-30 holiday in Tenerife leaving Stanstead on the ninth?

ANITA: No. Sorry.

CAROL COUGHS INTO HER HAND AND BLOWS IT TOWARDS ANITA, WHO RECOILS WHEN IT REACHES HER.

I've got a lovely cruise on the ship where they filmed *The Poseidon Adventure*

MARJORIE DAWES/FATFIGHTERS – PREGNANT PAT

INT: FATFIGHTERS.

TOM V/O: Because of the fat people, Britain is slowly sinking into the sea. An overweight woman in Great Yarmouth recently ate a whole packet of custard creams and half of Norfolk went under.

MARJORIE IS STANDING BY A TABLE WITH A FEW ITEMS ON IT. BY EACH ITEM IS A LITTLE SIGN WITH FAT CONTENT AND CALORIE COUNT. THE ITEMS INCLUDE A SMALL TREE BRANCH, A BAR OF SOAP, A BALL OF STRING, A LIGHT BULB. MARJORIE POINTS TO AN OLD PLIMSOLL.

MARJORIE: Right, that's about all we've got time for today –

PAT: Ooh, Marjorie?

MARJORIE: Yes, my sweet?

Ooh, I've got one... 'Jabba'.

EPISODE

PAT: Just to say me and Paul have had some good news. I've just found out that I'm pregnant.

THE GROUP OFFER THEIR CONGRATULATIONS.

MARJORIE: Are you sure or have you just been scoffing?

PAUL: Yeah, she's three months gone now so we're allowed to tell people. I've got the scan picture here.

PAT SMILES EXCITEDLY. PAUL TAKES THE PICTURE OUT. THE GROUP CRANE THEIR NECKS TO GET A GOOD LOOK.

GROUP: Oooh.

MARJORIE TAKES THE PICTURE FROM PAUL.

MARJORIE: You gonna keep it?

PAT: Sorry?

MARJORIE: You're not gonna get rid of it?

PAT: (PRETURBED) No, of course not.

MARJORIE: Ooh. Bit selfish of you.

PAUL: For God's sake.

THE GROUP ARE MURMURING THEIR DISCONTENT.

MARJORIE: No, FatFighters. I'm only thinking of the baby. You know, that poor baby is gonna be born a cake addict. It's gonna come out and straightaway it's gonna have to go through cold chicken.

PAT: Well, I'm gonna watch what I eat, now that I'm having a baby.

MARJORIE: Are you sure it's just the one? By the look of you you're gonna have a whole litter?

PAT: (RESTRAINED) We're just having the one.

MARJORIE STUDIES THE SCAN PICTURE.

MARJORIE: It looks fat already.

PAUL SNATCHES THE PICTURE FROM MARJORIE.

PAUL: (PROUD BUT HURT) It's beautiful. It's our little baby.

THERE'S A LULL IN THE ROOM. TANYA BREAKS IT.

TANYA: (TO PAT AND PAUL) Do you know what you're gonna call it?

PAUL: It's a 'he' and, no, we haven't decided on a name.

MARJORIE: Ooh, I know, this could be a little bit of fun here. Why don't we all try and think of names for the baby? Yeah, that'd be nice.

MARJORIE GOES AND STANDS BY THE WHITE BOARD. PAT AND PAUL EXCHANGE A LOOK. SHE WRITES 'BABY NAMES.' THERE ARE MURMURS OF EXCITEMENT IN THE ROOM.

MARJORIE: Right. What should they call it?

MEERA PUTS HER HAND UP

MARJORIE: Meera?

MEERA: John.

MARJORIE: What's that, my love?

MEERA: John.

MARJORIE: What's that, my love?

MEERA: John.

MARJORIE: What's that, my love?

MEERA: John.

MARJORIE: What's that, my love?

MEERA: John.

MARJORIE: What's that, my love?

MEERA: John.

MARJORIE: What's that, my love?

MEERA: John.

MARJORIE: What's that, my love?

MEERA: John.

What's that, my love?

MARJORIE: What's that, my love?

PAUL: (SIGHS) John!

MARJORIE: John! That's a nice name. John.

MARJORIE WRITES 'JOHN' ON THE BOARD.

MARJORIE: Anyone else? Tanya.

TANYA: Michael.

MARJORIE WRITES 'MICHAEL' ON THE BOARD.

PAT: Oh, that's a nice one.

TANYA: It's my husband's name.

MARJORIE: Oh yeah. The one who left you 'cause you got so fat. (TO PAT AND PAUL) Looking at you two, I can't really see it being a Michael or a John.

MARJORIE: Ooh, I've got one.

MARJORIE WRITES SOMETHING ON THE BOARD. WE REVEAL IT IS...

MARJORIE: 'Jabba'.

Fat Fighters

DIET BOOK

Remember, You can do it
if you don't chew it

SID/NEIGHBOUR WATCH – GYPSIES

EXT: SID'S HOUSE.

TOM V/O: Here in Grumble, Sid Pegg has called a meeting of Neighbour Watch.

WE SEE THE RESIDENTS LEAVING THEIR HOMES TO ATTEND THE MEETING. A UNION JACK LOOMS ABOVE THEM ON A FLAGPOLE. THERE IS A SIGN FOR 'LARCHWOOD CLOSE' OUTSIDE THE HOUSE. SID PEGG STANDS BY HIS FRONT DOOR USHERING HIS NEIGHBOURS IN QUICKLY.

INT: SID'S SUBURBAN HOUSE/LIVING ROOM. THERE ARE VARIOUS 'NEIGHBOUR WATCH' POSTERS AND LEAFLETS ON DISPLAY, AS WELL AS A SIGNED PICTURE OF EDWARD WOODWARD AS 'THE EQUALISER'. A FEW NEIGHBOURS ARE SAT AS SID TALKS. AMONG THEM ARE GILLIAN, A MIDDLE-AGED VICAR; DEAN AND HIS PREGNANT PARTNER CAROLINE, BOTH IN THEIR EARLY TWENTIES; LLOYD SNOW, AN UNASSUMING-LOOKING MAN IN HIS FORTIES. SID CLOSES THE CURTAINS.

SID: Right. Welcome to tonight's Neighbour Watch. Thank you all for coming at short notice but I felt we had to have an emergency meeting.

DEAN: What's happened?

LLOYD: I hadn't heard anything.

CAROLINE: Is there a problem?

SID: Yes, there is a problem. Our old friend the gypsy has moved into the close.

LLOYD: Where are they?

SID: Bleedin' bloody hell, Lloyd! They're only campin' out on your front lawn.

LLOYD: No, that's our caravan. Me and Susan just bought it.

THE GROUP SIGHS. ONE OR TWO GET UP TO LEAVE.

SID: Stay where you are! (THINKING ON HIS FEET) We still need to be on our guard against the gypsy threat! There are swarms of them.

WOMAN: (OOV) Shall I put the Findus Crispy Pancakes in?

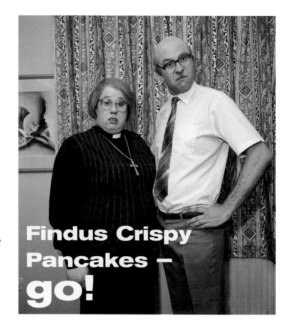

Findus Crispy Pancakes – go!

SID: (CALLS) Yes, wife. Findus Crispy Pancakes – go! (TO GROUP) So how do we spot a gypsy? A gypo. A gypolata. Watch and learn.

SID TURNS ON A PROJECTOR. ON A SCREEN WE SEE AN IMAGE OF DAVID ESSEX, IN THE SITCOM *THE RIVER*. SID HAS A POINTER.

SID: Number One. Your classic gypsy. Earring, neckerchief, waistcoat and a look in his eye that says 'I am going to tarmac your drive.' Number two...

THE SECOND SLIDE IS OF JOE LONGTHORNE.

SID: Gypsy Joe Longthorne. A sly fox. Uses many different voices. But mainly Shirley Bassey.

THE THIRD SLIDE IS OF THE MUSIC GROUP THE GYPSY KINGS.

SID: Number three. The Gypsy Kings. The actual Kings of the Gypsies. Last seen on *Sunday Sunday with Gloria Hunniford* in nineteen eighty-eight. But beware, they could be back in the charts at any moment.

SID: Now we know the enemy. Britain fights back. (CALLS) Wife?

WOMAN: (OOV) Yes?

SID: (CALLS) Bachelor's Super Noodles – Go! Mini Kievs on standby! (TO ALL) So what do we do if a gypsy – or a herd of gypsies, as I believe they are known – turn up on your doorstep? Can I have a volunteer please?

EPISODE

Number One.
Your classic gypsy.

EVERYBODY LOOKS DOWN, AVOIDING EYE CONTACT.

SID: Lloyd. I saw your hand go up.

LLOYD RELUCTANTLY GETS UP.

SID: Thank you, Lloyd. Little Lloyd. I don't know if you know but Lloyd was actually a contestant on *The Weakest Link.*

LLOYD: (WEARY) Yes.

SID: Right. A quick demo. Nstration. Right Lloyd, you are the gypsy. The gypmeister. The gypola.

GILLIAN: I must say I do think it's very offensive to talk about gypsies in this way.

SID: Good point, Mrs Vicar. Let's not be racialist. (TO LLOYD) So, you're the filthy gypsy and you are going to ask me if I wanna buy any clothes-pegs.

LLOYD: (SIGHS) Do I have to?

SID: You know, Lloyd, you've got very arrogant since you were on BBC 2.

LLOYD: Sorry. I'll be the gypsy then. 'Hello. Would you like to buy some –'

SUDDENLY SID PUSHES HIS FACE AND HOLDS IT.

SID: 'No, gypsy! No!' And it's as simple as that. (RAISES FIST IN THE AIR) Britain fights back.

SID RELEASES HIS GRIP. A RUFFLED LLOYD RETURNS TO HIS SEAT.

SID: Thank you, Lloyd. You are the weaker link. Goodbye. (CHUCKLES TO HIMSELF) The weaker link, goodbye... (TO GROUP) Right. Now. That's gypsies covered. Next... asylum seekers.

A PICTURE OF THE CHEEKY GIRLS COMES UP.

SID: No! We will not touch your bums. (CALLS) Wife. Butterscotch Angel Delight. Go!

DAFYDD — ELECTION

EXT: HIGH STREET. DAFYDD IS WALKING PURPOSEFULLY ALONG,
HOLDING A CLIPBOARD AND SOME LEAFLETS. HE IS DRESSED IN
CUSTOMISED PINSTRIPE SUIT AND PINK ROSETTE. DAFYDD HANDS
A LEAFLET TO AN ELDERLY COUPLE. A CAR PASSES BY WITH 'VOTE
PLAID CYMRU' ON IT. WE HEAR A MAN'S VOICE COMING FROM
A TANNOY ON THE ROOF OF THE CAR...

TANNOY: Vote Noel Hopkins in tomorrow's election.

TOM V/O: Here in the charming Welsh village of
Llandewi Breffi, bottom enthusiast Dafydd Thomas
is standing for election.

EXT: DOORWAY/MRS TEALE'S HOUSE. DAFYDD SHAKES HIS HEAD AND STRIDES UP TO
THE FRONT DOOR. HE KNOCKS ON THE DOOR. IT IS OPENED BY A FRIENDLY-
LOOKING OLD LADY, MRS TEALE.

MRS TEALE: Hello, Dafydd.

DAFYDD: Good afternoon, Mrs Teale. I was
just wondering if I can count on your vote tomorrow?

MRS TEALE: Oh. Are you standing in the by-election?

DAFYDD: It's not just a bi-election, Mrs Teale. It's for gays and
straights too. Anyone can vote, regardless of sexuality. Honestly,
it's like banging your head against a brick wall!

MRS TEALE: So who are you standing for?

DAFYDD: The Gay Rights For Gays party.

MRS TEALE: Oh that's nice.

DAFYDD: Anyway, seeing as I am the only gay in the village I
shouldn't think anyone will be remotely interested. Good day.

MRS TEALE: Oh no, lots of folk round here drop anchor in Pooh
Bay. Is that your manifesto? Let's have a look, then.

DAFYDD HANDS MRS TEALE A LITTLE PINK PAMPHLET. MRS TEALE STUDIES IT WHILE
DAFYDD SPEAKS.

DAFYDD: If I am elected I promise to turn the park into a
twenty-four hour gay cruising zone.

MRS TEALE: Yes?

DAFYDD: I shall be knocking down the old folks' home and building a gay sauna.

MRS TEALE: (READING) 'Hotbots'?

DAFYDD: That's right. And I shall be erecting two statues on the village green, there, of Colin and Justin.

MRS TEALE: Oh, I love their shows.

DAFYDD: Oh do you indeed? Well let me tell you this, Mrs Homophobe. I was watching *Makeover Madness* only this morning and I have very strong suspicions that at least one of them is a gay.

MRS TEALE: Oh no, I think they're both full-time bummers.

DAFYDD: (GRIMACING) Well, anyway, thank you for your time, Mrs Teale.

MRS TEALE: Good luck, Dafydd. You can count on my support.

DAFYDD: Really?

MRS TEALE: Oh yes. I'm all for Gay Rights. In fact I myself drink from the furry cup.

DAFYDD FAINTS.

MRS TEALE: Dafydd?

'Hotbots'?

EPISODE

LINDA – TURBAN

INT: LINDA'S OFFICE.

TOM V/O: In her office, university lecturer Linda Flint is meeting a student. I very nearly got into university... but Security managed to stop me.

LINDA SITS OPPOSITE A MAN WITH A TURBAN (STEVE).

LINDA: ...So that's the problem, is it?

STEVE: Yeah, and there aren't any copies of *The Female Eunuch* left in the library so I can't really write the essay.

LINDA: Oh, well I've got a copy here –

LINDA HOLDS UP A COPY.

STEVE: Great.

LINDA: But that's mine and I don't want to lend it out. Martin may have one in his office.

LINDA PICKS UP THE PHONE.

LINDA: Martin, it's Linda. I've got a student here who wants to know if he can borrow your copy of *The Female Eunuch*. Steve. You know Steve. He's got a beard. Quite tall. Have you ever seen *It Ain't Half Hot, Mum*? No. Looks like he's just stepped out of the shower. Think Carmen Miranda without the fruit. That's right. Ali Bongo. (TO STEVE) He says go straight up.

STEVE: My name's not Ali Bongo.

LINDA: Sorry. Steve, yes. Steve Bongo.

My name's not Ali Bongo.

MR MANN – ROY'S NEWS

INT: ROY'S MAGAZINES.

TOM V/O: Newspapers and magazines are very popular in Britain. The first magazine ever published was in 1502... What Hi-Fi.

MR MANN ENTERS AND APPROACHES THE COUNTER, BUT NOWHERE NEAR WHERE ROY IS STANDING.

MR MANN: Do you work here?

ROY: (MOVING TO FACE MR MANN) Yes, I do. Can I be of assistance?

MR MANN: Hello. I'd like to buy a magazine please.

ROY: Well, we've got lots here.

MR MANN: Do you have *Bad Feet Monthly*?

ROY: Er, no. I don't think so.

MR MANN: *Athlete's Foot Times*?

ROY: Sorry.

MR MANN: *Verucca Today*?

ROY: I don't think we do.

MR MANN: *What Bunion*?

ROY: No.

MR MANN: *Ingrowing Toenail Weekly*?

ROY: I've not heard of that one.

MR MANN: You get a free binder with part one and a sachet of toenail clippings.

ROY: I can't help you, I'm afraid.

MR MANN: Do you have any magazines devoted to problem feet?

ROY: I'm not sure. One moment. (CALLS) Margaret? Margaret?

LONG PAUSE. ROY AND MR MANN FIND NEARBY SEATS AND SIT DOWN. THEY PULL OUT A BOOK EACH AND START READING.

MARGARET: Yes?

THE PAIR STOP READING, STAND UP AND RESUME POSITIONS.

ROY: There's a gentleman here wants to know if we have any magazines devoted to problem feet.

MR MANN: Not *Celebrity Callus Monthly*. I already have that one.

ROY: Not *Celebrity Callus Monthly*. He already has that one.

MARGARET: I'm not sure. If we do have any they'll be in the General Interest section.

ROY: Right, let's have a look.

ROY HAS A LOOK.

ROY: I can't see any, Margaret.

MARGARET: Just across from *What Binliner?*

ROY: Right...

MARGARET: Next to the *Molester's Review*.

ROY: Oh, thank you very much, Margaret. Yes, I've found it. It was tucked just behind *Out Of Date Crisps Periodical*.

ROY PULLS OUT A MAGAZINE. WE SEE THAT IT IS CALLED *FOOT AND ANKLE PAIN BONANZA*.

ROY: There you go.

MR MANN: (READS) *Foot And Ankle Pain Bonanza*.

MARGARET: Well, Roy? What does he reckon?

ROY: Well, myself? What do you reckon?

MR MANN: I am not going to buy this magazine I am afraid.

ROY: Oh, what a surprise. Any particular reason?

MR MANN: I'm not interested in ankle pain. I am only really concerned with foot pain.

ROY: Oh. Do you suffer from foot pain?

MR MANN: No.

ROY: Are there any magazines here that interest you?

MR MANN: *Hello* magazine.

ROY: Now we're talking.

ROY PICKS UP A COPY OF *HELLO* MAGAZINE.

MR MANN: No, I was just saying hello to that magazine over there.

ROY: (FLATLY) I hate you so much.

MR MANN: I know.

SEBASTIAN AND MICHAEL — THE MOUSTACHE

TOM V/O: At number 10 Downing Street a group of trade union leaders are presenting a petition calling for the Prime Minister's resignation.

EXT: NO 10 DOWNING STREET. A SMALL GROUP OF SERIOUS-LOOKING TRADE UNION LEADERS ARRIVE AND RING THE BELL. SEBASTIAN OPENS THE DOOR. ONE OF THE LEADERS HANDS HIM A PETITION. SEBASTIAN LEAFS THROUGH IT DISDAINFULLY, RIPS IT UP AND THROWS IT BACK AT THEM BEFORE CLOSING THE DOOR.

INT: PM'S OFFICE. MICHAEL HAS HIS BACK TURNED AND IS LEAFING THROUGH SOME FILES. SEBASTIAN ENTERS.

SEBASTIAN: Morning, Prime Minister.

MICHAEL: Morning, Sebastian.

SEBASTIAN: Did you have a nice holiday?

MICHAEL: Very nice, thank you.

SEBASTIAN: I've got the draft budget from the Chancellor here.

MICHAEL: Thank you, Sebastian.

MICHAEL TURNS ROUND. WE SEE HE HAS A MOUSTACHE.

SEBASTIAN: (SHOCKED) Urgh!

MICHAEL: What's the matter?

SEBASTIAN: (POINTING) What's that?

MICHAEL: Oh... moustache. I grew it on holiday.

SEBASTIAN: I don't like it.

MICHAEL: Sarah loves it.

SEBASTIAN: I don't.

MICHAEL: Why not?

SEBASTIAN: It tickles when you kiss.

MICHAEL: We're not going to kiss.

Looks fishy, doesn't he?

SEBASTIAN: Not today, no, but if we were to kiss, for whatever reason, I'd prefer for you not to have the moustache.

SARAH BREEZES IN.

SARAH: Darling, did I leave my Women's Institute speech in here?

MICHAEL: Yes darling, it's here, it's very good.

SARAH: Oh, thank you. Hello Sebastian.

SEBASTIAN: Whatever.

SARAH: What do you think of the moustache? Looks dishy, doesn't he?

SEBASTIAN: I don't know. I'm not gay.

SARAH: I think it looks great, and I think the voters will love it.

SEBASTIAN: I don't think they will. I don't think they'll vote for you any more.

MICHAEL: People don't just vote for me because they like the way I look. They vote for me because they like my policies, don't they?

SEBASTIAN DOES A BIG PERFORMANCE OF LOOKING UNCERTAIN.

SARAH: Right, well I've got to dash, darling. I'll be late.

SARAH KISSES HIM. SEBASTIAN SCREWS UP HIS NOSE.

SEBASTIAN: (MUTTERS) Get a room.

SARAH EXITS.

MICHAEL: Sebastian, I've called off all my other meetings this afternoon, so you and I can thrash out this budget proposal together.

SEBASTIAN SHRUGS.

SEBASTIAN: Not bothered now.

MICHAEL: Oh. You said you loved it when we work closely together.

SEBASTIAN: Yeah. Yeah, I did. But... moustache.

MICHAEL: Oh, well if that's the way you feel, I'll get someone else. (ON INTERCOM) Could you ask Gregory to come up to my office please?

SECRETARY: Yes, Prime Minister.

MICHAEL: Thank you. (TO SEBASTIAN) By the way, Sarah's away at the weekend. I thought you and I could go down to Chequers and work on this election together.

SEBASTIAN: (SIGHS) I don't fancy you.

GREGORY ENTERS.

GREGORY: Morning Sebastian. Prime Minister.

MICHAEL: Morning Gregory.

GREGORY: (BRIGHTENS) Oh I love the moustache.

SEBASTIAN: Have 'im.

SEBASTIAN FLOUNCES OUT

Have 'im.

MAGGIE AND JUDY — DOG WALKING

TOM V/O: In the charming village of Pox, just outside Little Stool, Judith Pike and Margaret Blackamoor are enjoying a walk.

EXT: VILLAGE GREEN. MAGGIE WALKS AN OLD ENGLISH SHEEPDOG ACROSS THE GREEN, ACCOMPANIED BY JUDY.

MAGGIE: ...and I'm sorry but I don't think women should be allowed to vote.

JUDY: Yes, I think I see your point. Oh, look. There's Marion. Hello Marion, dear.

MARION APPROACHES. SHE WALKS A SMALL CHINESE-LOOKING DOG.

MARION: Hello ladies. Lovely dog.

MAGGIE: Thank you. George, yes, he's an old English sheepdog. Pure pedigree.

MARION: He's lovely.

MAGGIE: Thank you. And yours is beautiful.

MAGGIE CROUCHES DOWN AND STROKES AND PATS MARION'S DOG.

MAGGIE: (TO DOG) Aren't you? Eh? Eh? (TO MARION) What's the breed?

MARION: She's a Chinese dog. A Shitsu.

MAGGIE STRAIGHTENS UP. JUDY LOOKS TO MAGGIE, AFRAID OF WHAT'S GOING TO HAPPEN. MAGGIE LOOKS PAINED AND ILL. WE THINK SHE MIGHT BE SICK.

JUDY: Maggie! No!

THEN GEORGE THROWS UP, ALL OVER THE SHITSU. GEORGE THROWS UP A LITTLE OVER MARION'S OPEN SANDALS. MARION IS AGHAST. WHEN THE TORRENT HAS ENDED…

MAGGIE: There's a good boy. Come along now!

MAGGIE LEADS GEORGE AWAY.

MAGGIE: See you at church on Sunday.

There's a good boy.

LOU AND ANDY – PYLON

TOM V/O: Frisbees were invented in 1928 by Society beauty Lady Lucinda Frisbee, to relieve the boredom between the wars.

EXT: FIELD. LOU STANDS A FEW PACES AWAY FROM ANDY WITH A FRISBEE. BEHIND THEM IS A PYLON. LOU GENTLY THROWS THE FRISBEE TO ANDY. IT LANDS ON HIS LAP.

LOU: Well done.

ANDY: What happens now?

LOU: You throw it back.

ANDY: Yeah, I know.

ANDY FEEBLY DROPS THE FRISBEE OFF HIS LAP. IT FALLS TO THE GROUND.

LOU: I didn't quite catch that one. You've got to really throw it.

LOU HANDS THE FRISBEE BACK TO ANDY.

ANDY: Yeah, I know.

ANDY HURLS THE FRISBEE. THE WIND TAKES IT UP ONTO THE PYLON.

LOU: Oh no. The frisbee is stuck up the pylon.

ANDY: Go and get it then.

LOU: Well, I can't. The pylon carries electric current – it would be very dangerous.

ANDY: (DREAMILY) Yeah, I know.

LOU: We'll have to leave it there. Let's think of another game to play.

ANDY: (FIRMLY) Want me frisbee.

LOU: Oh God, I'll see if I can find someone to help. You wait there.

LOU WANDERS OFF TO FIND SOMEONE. A FARMER APPROACHES.

LOU: Excuse me, are you the farmer?

FARMER: Yes I am.

IN THE BACKGROUND ANDY GETS OUT OF HIS CHAIR, RUNS OVER TO THE PYLON, AND STARTS CLIMBING IT CONFIDENTLY.

LOU: We've got a little problem. We've got a Frisbee stuck up a pylon.

FARMER: Yeah, but I've just come to tell you, this is private property. This is my field, mate.

LOU: My friend here is in a wheelchair, and he likes nothing more than a game of Frisbee. He loves playing the Frisbee, that's him.

FARMER: I realise, yeah.

LOU: I imagine you'd need a pole attached to another pole attached to another pole, wouldn't you.

ANDY GETS QUITE NEAR THE FRISBEE. HE TOUCHES A COIL AND STARTS SHAKING. WE SEE BLUE SPARKS FLYING FROM HIM AND SOME SMOKE.

FARMER: Sorry about that.

LOU: Well, thank you very much, you've been very helpful. Goodbye.

FARMER: Bye.

LOU WALKS BACK TO WHERE THE WHEELCHAIR IS.

LOU: Nice man.

ANDY IS NOW SITTING BACK IN HIS CHAIR, BLACK AND SMOKING, WITH HIS HAIR STANDING ON END.

LOU: Oh... it came down, did it? Good.

LOU WHEELS ANDY OFF INTO THE DISTANCE.

LOU: There's a strange smell of burning fat.

ANDY: (IN RASPY CROAKING VOICE) Yeah, I know.

TOM V/O: Alas, our journey round Little Britain is at an end; what an illuminating voyage it has been. I must go now as I'm just about to reach orgasm. Good cry.

There's a strange smell of burning fat.

Dr Lawrence's

Michael's still life painting is a beautiful representation of his newfound peace of mind. As you may know, Michael is leaving us soon and I think he could go on to become a very successful artist. As long as he stops biting people.

I really like Susan's fruit bowl. The colours and textures are rich and vibrant and I think this shows Susan's growing optimism about returning to the outside world. Well done, Susan. You're nearly there. You just need to start wearing clothes now.

Art Therapy Class

Once again Anne has excelled herself. The fruit is so vividly realised it is as if you can reach out and touch it. I asked Anne which artists had inspired her. Was it Van Gogh, Picasso or Rembrandt, to which she replied simply 'eh eh eh' before placing one of her droppings into her hand. I think she may be ready to go home.

TOM V/O: Britain, Britain, Britain, we have exported so many great things around the world: slavery, hooliganism, and Starlight Express. But none of this would have been possible without the people of Britain. Today now we look at what they, whom boom boom, let me hear you say way-oh, way-oh, bring it on!

LOU AND ANDY — PATIO

TOM V/O: It's half past Mr Ernest Ndukwe and Lou and Andy are on their way home from the shops.

EXT: STREET. LOU RECOGNISES A PASSING WOMAN AND STOPS TO CHAT. ANDY LIFTS UP HER SKIRT TO HAVE A LOOK. FINISHING HIS CHAT, LOU WHEELS HIM OFF, TOTALLY OBLIVIOUS.

EXT: ANDY'S GARDEN/PATIO. LOU, IN OVERALLS, IS PUTTING THE FINISHING TOUCHES TO A LARGE AREA OF PATIO (HALF THE GARDEN). ANDY SITS, EATING SOME CHEAP BISCUITS.

LOU: This patio is going to look lovely. You're going to be able to sit out here in the summer and sunbathe.

ANDY: Yeah I know.

LOU: Right. Nearly finished.

ANDY: I wanna go on it now.

LOU: No, you can't go on it now. It's got to dry first.

ANDY: Yeah I know.

LOU: Oh no, you can't go on it now. It's got to dry first.

ANDY: Yeah I know.

LOU GRABS HIS BACK.

LOU: Ooh. Ow. Ooh me back. Oooh. Ah. Something went there. It went the other day as well, you know, when I carried you up the top of Post Office Tower.

LOU TURNS AWAY FROM ANDY AND STRETCHES HIS BACK. IN THE BACKGROUND ANDY GETS UP, WALKS TO THE CENTRE OF THE WET CEMENT, LIES DOWN TO SUNBATHE FOR A MOMENT, SIGHS WITH BOREDOM, GETS UP (COVERED IN CEMENT) AND RETURNS TO HIS SEAT. LOU COMPLETES HIS STRETCHES AND TURNS ROUND TO SEE A MASSIVE IMPRINT IN THE CEMENT.

LOU: Who done that?!

ANDY: A bird.

Computer says no.

CAROL — INSURANCE

TOM V/O: At this travel agents, Carol Beer is once again working her nuts off.

EXT: 'SUNSEARCHERS' TRAVEL AGENTS. WE SEE CAROL BEER INSIDE THE SHOP, STANDING AT THE WINDOW. SHE PINS UP A POSTER THAT READS 'BASRAH - HALF BOARD - £129'.

INT: TRAVEL AGENTS. CAROL BEER IS SAT AT HER DESK. IN FRONT OF HER IS A FRIENDLY MIDDLE-AGED COUPLE (ROBERT AND WENDY).

ROBERT: So that flight leaves Heathrow on the eighth?

CAROL: Yes.

CAROL TYPES.

CAROL: Will you be taking your wife on as hand luggage?

ROBERT: No.

CAROL: Oh. So you'll need two seats.

CAROL TYPES.

CAROL: That's all booked for you.

WENDY: Ooh I forgot to ask. Does that include insurance?

CAROL TYPES.

CAROL: Computer says no.

WENDY: I think we should take some out.

CAROL: We do offer a very reasonable insurance package here at Sunsearchers.

ROBERT: And that covers us against accidents, does it?

CAROL TYPES.

CAROL: Computer says no.

We offer more comprehensive insurance, for an extra fee.

ROBERT: Oh. So it just covers us against theft?

CAROL DRAGS HER FINGER ACROSS A ROW OF KEYS.

CAROL: Computer says no.

ROBERT: Medical bills?

CAROL TYPES

CAROL: Computer would like to refer the honourable gentleman to the answer it gave some moments ago.

WENDY: Doesn't sound like it'll be much use.

CAROL: No.

WENDY: We'll leave it thanks.

CAROL: We do offer Sunsearchers platinum gold insurance.

WENDY: Oh yes?.

ROBERT: What kind of things does that cover?

CAROL: Well, last week we had a man in Barbados who lost a flip-flop. We were able to send a replacement flip-flop out to him, first class.

WENDY: Really?

CAROL: All he had to do was cover the cost of the flight. And the flip-flop.

ROBERT: I think we'll forget about the insurance, thank you.

CAROL: (RESIGNED) I'll just give you your tickets, then.

CAROL PUTS THE TICKETS INTO AN ENVELOPE THEN COUGHS INTO IT BEFORE THE ENVELOPE OVER. THE COUPLE LOOK INTO THE ENVELOPE AND CAROL'S COUGH ECHOES BACK AT THEM.

VICKY POLLARD — BABYSITTER 1

INT: RICHARD & JENNIFER'S HOUSE/LIVING ROOM

TOM v/o: It's half past Queen and Paul Rogers, and in Poop this couple are getting ready to go out.

A VERY TASTEFULLY FURNISHED LARGE LIVING ROOM OF A TOWN HOUSE. A MIDDLE-CLASS COUPLE IN THEIR THIRTIES, JENNIFER AND RICHARD, ARE ADDING FINAL TOUCHES TO THEIR OUTFITS.

RICHARD: Darling? Darling, have you seen my wallet?

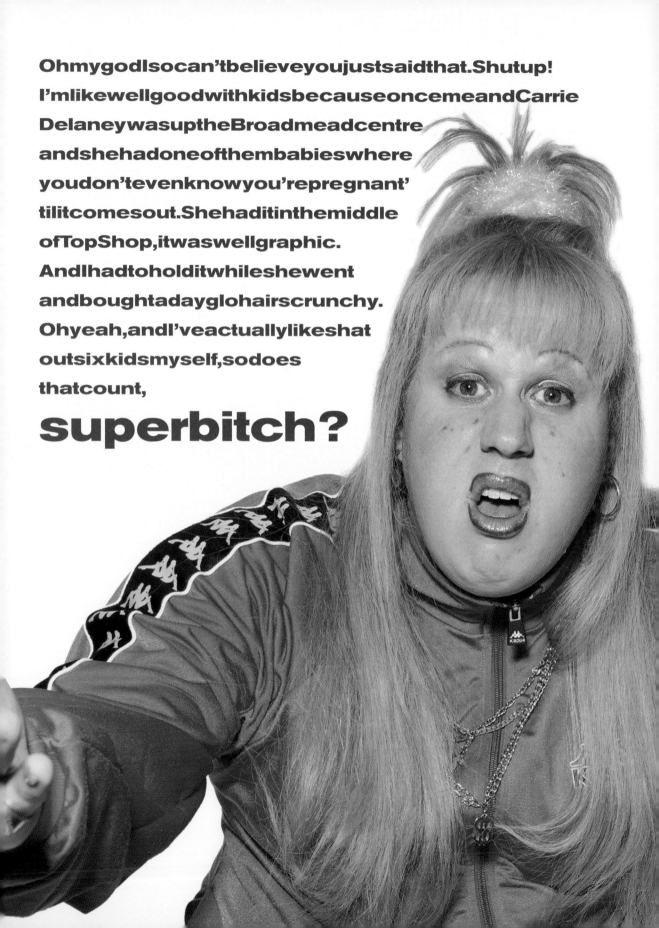

OhmygodIsocan'tbelieveyoujustsaidthat.Shutup!
I'mlikewellgoodwithkidsbecauseoncemeandCarrie
DelaneywasuptheBroadmeadcentre
andshehadoneofthembabieswhere
youdon'tevenknowyou'repregnant'
tilitcomesout.Shehaditinthemiddle
ofTopShop,itwaswellgraphic.
AndIhadtoholditwhileshewent
andboughtadayglohairscrunchy.
Ohyeah,andI'veactuallylikeshat
outsixkidsmyself,sodoes
thatcount,

superbitch?

JENNIFER: (DESCENDING) It's by the phone. So, aren't you going to tell me how I look?

RICHARD: Beautiful.

THE DOORBELL RINGS.

RICHARD: Ah. That'll be the babysitter. I'll get it.

RICHARD OPENS THE DOOR. VICKY IS STANDING THERE.

RICHARD: Hello. You must be Victoria.

VICKY: No but yeah but no but yeah but no cos I'm totally like the babysitter or summin' or nuffin'.

RICHARD: Come in. You're a little late.

VICKY: Don't go givin' me evils!

VICKY ENTERS, TALKING AS SHE WALKS.

VICKY: What happened was was I was gonna get here about a half hour ago but I couldn't because we was all at McDonald's 'cause Jade Maguire really fancies this bloke who works there called Lee Cherry who used to go to our school and he's done like the best out of everyone in his year, 'cause he's got two stars on his name badge, one for slicing gherkins and the other for moppin' up piss. Anyway Shanita told Lee that Jade really fancied him and then Jade took Lee round the back of the deep fat fryer and showed him her Egg McMuffins.

JENNIFER IS WAITING FOR VICKY TO STOP SPEAKING.

JENNIFER: Hello there. I'm Jennifer.

JENNIFER HOLDS OUT HER HAND. VICKY TURNS AWAY AND WALKS TO THEIR DRINKS.

VICKY: Got any Pernod?

THE COUPLE LOOK AT EACH OTHER UNCERTAINLY.

JENNIFER: Archie's already in bed. He should be fine. If he wakes up, don't let him watch cartoons.

RICHARD: Yes, he'll settle better if you read him a book.

VICKY: A what?

JENNIFER: I hope you don't mind me asking but have you looked after children much before?

VICKY: Oh my God I so can't believe you just said that. Shut up! I'm like well good with kids because once me and Carrie Delaney was up the Broadmead centre and she had one of them babies where you don't even know you're pregnant 'til it comes out. She had it in the middle of Top Shop, it was well graphic. And I had to hold it while she went and bought a day-glo hair scrunchy. Oh yeah, and I've actually like shat out six kids myself, so does that count, superbitch?

VICKY SITS DOWN.

JENNIFER: So who's looking after them tonight?

VICKY: I don't know!

RICHARD AND JENNIFER SMILE A LITTLE NERVOUSLY. FROM OUTSIDE WE HEAR A HORN TOOT.

RICHARD: Taxi's here.

RICHARD AND JENNIFER MAKE FOR THE DOOR.

JENNIFER: You will be okay?

VICKY: Yeah! God! Stop getting involved!

JENNIFER WINCES. RICHARD USHERS HER OUT. VICKY POURS A DRINK AND PICKS UP THE TV REMOTE CONTROL. SHE FLICKS THROUGH THE CHANNELS.

ARCHIE: (OOV) Mummy?

VICKY: (DEEP VOICE) Shut up!

Got any Pernod?

AnywayShanitatoldLeethatJade
reallyfanciedhimandthenJadetook
Leeroundthebackofthedeepfatfrye
randshowedhimherEggMcMuffins.

LINDA — MOLE

INT: LINDA'S OFFICE.

TOM V/O: Like most universities in Britain this one offers a variety of courses, including a post-grad on the life and work of Jayne Middlemiss.

LINDA SITS OPPOSITE MOLLY, A YOUNG GIRL WITH A LARGE MOLE ABOVE HER LIP.

MOLLY: I just wondered if you know what the deadline is for the Sylvia Plath essay.

LINDA: Oh, aren't her poems wonderful? She always seems a bit down in the dumps though.

MOLLY: I love 'The Bell-jar'.

LINDA: I read it. I thought 'Cheer up love, might never happen.' Have you tried Jilly Cooper?

MOLLY: No. Sorry, I just need to know when the deadline is.

LINDA: I'm not sure. Martin'll know.

LINDA PICKS UP THE PHONE AND DIALS.

LINDA: Martin, it's Linda. I've got Molly Spencer here. Wants to know when the Plath essay is due in. Molly. You know Molly. Lovely brown hair. Quite petite. Almost very pretty. Looks like she's balancing a Malteser on her face. When you see her you want to shout 'Careful, there's a bee on your...' and then you realise. That's right – Molly The Mole.

'I am a mole and I live in a hole.'

LINDA PUTS THE PHONE DOWN.

LINDA: It's Thursday.

MOLLY: Thanks very much.

MOLLY GETS UP TO LEAVE.

LINDA: (SINGS TO HERSELF) 'I am a mole and I live in a hole.'

SIR NORMAN FRY — GAYDAR

TOM V/O: It's half past Mr Miyagi and once again Sir Norman Fry MP has some explaining to do.

EXT: COUNTRY ESTATE. SIR NORMAN FRY, ARMS BY HIS SIDE WITH HIS WIFE CAMILLA AND THEIR YOUNG SON AND DAUGHTER APPROACH THE GATE AT THE END OF THE DRIVE. WAITING FOR THEM IS A LARGE GROUP OF JOURNALISTS, PHOTOGRAPHERS AND TV CREWS. SIR NORMAN TAKES OUT A PIECE OF PAPER.

SIR NORMAN: I have a statement I would like to read. Last week, I purchased a new camera and whilst in my office in the House of Commons I accidentally took a picture of myself naked. That picture somehow – and I would love to know how – found its way onto Gaydar, which I later discovered to be a dating web site for sodomites. Basically you pay a flat fee, post your stats online and then... (CHECKS HIMSELF) I was then invited to join a group of gentlemen at a party in Brighton where I was planning to give a talk about education reforms. However, shortly after my arrival my clothes accidentally fell off. At that moment I slipped on a glacé cherry and landed inside one of the men. As far as I am concerned that is the end of the matter. Thank you.

SIR NORMAN GOES TO KISS HIS WIFE FOR THE CAMERAS. SHE TURNS AWAY AND LEADS THE CHILDREN BACK TO THE HOUSE. SIR NORMAN FOLLOWS.

PRESS: Sir Norman! Sir Norman! Will you be resigning?

At that moment I slipped on a glacé cherry and landed inside one of the men.

Press Statement – 11/10/05

Last week, I purchased a new camera and whilst in my office in the House of Commons I accidentally took a picture of myself naked.

That picture somehow – and I would love to know how – found its way onto Gaydar, which I later discovered to be a dating web site for sodomites.

I was then invited to join a group of gentlemen at a party in Brighton where I was planning to give a talk about education reforms.

However, shortly after my arrival my clothes fell off. At that moment I slipped on a glacé cherry and landed inside one of the men.

As far as I am concerned that is the end of the matter.

Thank you.

The Fry Family Estate
Lower Bank Lane, Crofton, Hertfordshire, HE4 5OP
Tel: 01632 960774 Fax: 01632 960773

MARJORIE DAWES/FATFIGHTERS — SLIDES

INT: FATFIGHTERS. THE GROUP ARE ASSEMBLED AS NORMAL. BEHIND MARJORIE IS A PROJECTION SCREEN. BEHIND THE GROUP IS A SLIDE PROJECTOR.

TOM V/O: Aren't fat people loathsome? Just look at their stupid fat faces. I'd like to give them all a punch on the nose. But I can't. I'm too fat.

MARJORIE: But what if we do get hungry between meals? Well, I have a little bit of low-fat cottage cheese on some Ryvita and you can have that as it is, or you can deep-fry it.

THE GROUP LOOK PUZZLED.

MARJORIE: Now today's buzzword is 'Motivisation'. Last week I asked you all to bring in a picture of yourself not looking at your best to act as an incentive next time you're reaching for that slice of cake. Ooh, we like cake, though, don't we. We like a bit of cake, don't we? Yeah. Cake. Gimme cake. Gimme cake, now. We like cake. We like cake. I like cake, though. I do. I just like cake. I like it a lot. I. Like. Cake. Gimme cake, gimme cake. (GERMAN ACCENT) I vant ze cake!

THE GROUP LOOK SUITABLY BAFFLED.

MARJORIE: So let's have a look at these pictures. Paul, can you dim the lights please?

PAUL DOES SO.

MARJORIE: Oh yeah, and I don't wanna hear any rustling. This is not an excuse to eat.

THE PROJECTOR IS TURNED ON. MARJORIE REMAINS BY THE SCREEN WITH A REMOTE CONTROL IN HER HAND.

MARJORIE: Let's have a look at the first photo, then.

IT'S A PICTURE OF MEERA POSING HAPPILY OUTSIDE HER SUBURBAN HOUSE. NEXT TO HER IS AN ASIAN MAN OF A SIMILAR AGE.

EPISODE

MARJORIE: Ooh, at home with the Kumars, ha ha. Have you seen that programme? It's actually very funny 'cause they're Asian. So where was this photo taken, my love? Was this in India, my love?

MEERA: New Malden.

MARJORIE: We'll never know. Tanya.

THE NEXT SLIDE. IT'S TANYA AT A PARTY, TUCKING IN TO A PLATEFUL OF BUFFET FOOD.

MARJORIE: Ooh, that took guts to bring that one in, my love. And where was this photo taken?

TANYA: It was at my sister's sixtieth.

MARJORIE: What, you mean you still get invited to family dos?

TANYA: Yeah.

MARJORIE: Oh. 'Cause if you were my sister, I would deny all knowledge of your existence, but I mean that in a caring way. Bless your over-worked heart.

MARJORIE CLICKS HER REMOTE CONTROL. WE SEE PAUL SMILING. IN THE BACKGROUND IS THE STATUE OF LIBERTY. HE WEARS A NEW YORK T-SHIRT AND BASEBALL CAP.

Bless your over-worked heart.

MARJORIE: Paul. Where was this?

PAUL: New York.

MARJORIE: Really? And did you pig out when you were there?

PAUL: Well, you know what it's like when you're on holiday.

MARJORIE: Yeah, well that's why you're here, Paul. Because you cannot control your binge eating. Excuse me for a moment, FatFighters.

MARJORIE CLICKS ON A BLANK THEN DISAPPEARS BEHIND THE SCREEN. IN SILHOUETTE WE SEE HER REACH INTO HER JACKET, PULL OUT A STRING OF SAUSAGES AND A FISH AND GUZZLE THEM DOWN IN SUPER QUICK TIME. RETRACTING THE FISH BONES FROM HER MOUTH, SHE BURPS THEN RETURNS.

MARJORIE: Just had to blow my nose. Right, let's have a look at the next picture.

PAT'S PICTURE APPEARS. SHE IS IN HER WEDDING DRESS STANDING NEXT TO PAUL.

MARJORIE: Oh mama you fat! (MOCK-SYMPATHETIC) So Pat, how does this picture make you feel, my darling?

PAT: Well, although it was a very happy day, as it was my wedding, I do think I look very large in that dress.

MARJORIE: Hmm, did they have to roll you down the aisle?

PAT: No, I walked.

MARJORIE: Brave. (TO PAUL) And, even though she looked like that you didn't have second thoughts? You still went through with it?

PAUL: Of course. (TO PAT) I look at Pat, and there's a beautiful person inside.

MARJORIE: There's a few of 'em.

MARJORIE: And now, because it's only fair, here is a picture of me not looking at my best.

IT IS JUST A PICTURE OF MARJORIE'S HEAD CRUDELY PUT ON A CATALOGUE MODEL'S BODY.

MARJORIE: I've lost a bit of weight since then, obviously. Lights on.

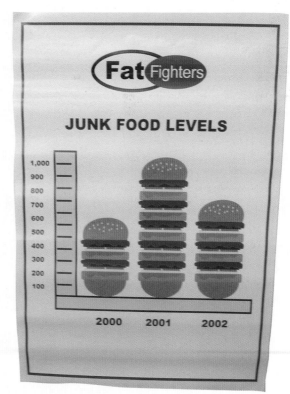

VICKY POLLARD – BABYSITTER 2

EXT: STREET/RICHARD AND JENNIFER'S HOUSE. JENNIFER AND RICHARD EXIT A TAXI. THEY NUZZLE AGAINST EACH OTHER.

RICHARD: (TO TAXI DRIVER) Keep the change.

JENNIFER: Hey – no yawning from you. The night isn't over yet!

THEY SHARE A SMILE. THE PAIR THEN NOTICE THERE IS LOUD MUSIC AND LOTS OF ACTIVITY COMING FROM THEIR HOUSE. SOMEONE COMES OUT TO BE SICK.

INT. RICHARD AND JENNIFER'S LIVING ROOM. THE ROOM IS IN A STATE OF UTTER CHAOS. FURNITURE, CURTAINS, PICTURES AND MIRRORS ARE ALL TRASHED. THERE IS A FIRE IN THE MIDDLE OF THE SOFA. AN OUT-OF-CONTROL TEENAGE PARTY IS TAKING PLACE. LOTS OF TEENAGERS IN TRACKSUITS ARE GETTING OFF WITH EACH OTHER. SOME BOYS ARE SPRAYING GRAFFITI ON THE WALL. VICKY IS GETTING OFF WITH A TEENAGE BOY.

JENNIFER: (FURIOUS) Vicky!

VICKY: What are you doing here? You ain't invited.

RICHARD: Where's Archie? Is he alright?

VICKY: Yeah. We sent him down the offy to get some more fags.

JENNIFER: What?!

VICKY: Don't go givin' me evils – we given him fake ID. Anyway I am actually quite busy at the moment tryin' to get off with this bloke actually if you don't mind actually!

RICHARD: (FURIOUS) Get out! Get out of my house!

VICKY: Don't worry. We're going. This party is like well sad anyway. (TO RICHARD) And I found your pornos, you dirty bastard.

VICKY HEADS FOR THE FRONT DOOR WITH HER FELLA IN TOW. RICHARD AND JENNIFER REMAIN IN THE LIVING ROOM, IN SHOCK, SURROUNDED BY THE CHAOS OF THE PARTY (WHICH IS STILL GOING ON). VICKY RETURNS.

VICKY: Oh yeah, and I can do next Tuesday if you want. Goin'!

THE HORSE WHISPERER

INT: COMPUTER SHOP.

TOM V/O: This is a computer shop. Computers date back to the reign of King Henry the Eighth. Computers then were very basic; you could only really get Pacman and Snoopy Tennis.

A MAN ENTERS THE SHOP WITH A BOX OF COMPUTER EQUIPMENT. WE SEE FROM THE INSTORE LEAFLETS THAT THE SHOP IS CALLED 'SHOP THAT SELLS COMPUTERS'. ASHRAF, AN ASSISTANT, IS ON THE TELEPHONE.

ASHRAF: ...did you see that *Pirates of the Caribbean?* That was the lamest movie, man. I did not like that. (ACKNOWLEDGES THE CUSTOMER) Yeah, wicked, I'll call you later. (TO CUSTOMER) Yes, boss?

CUSTOMER: Yeah, I bought an XP upgrade for my laptop but it hasn't installed right.

ASHRAF: Okay, let's take a look at it then.

ASHRAF PRESSES A FEW KEYS.

ASHRAF: Yeah. This is XP Professional, though, innit, not the home edition.

CUSTOMER: Yeah.

ASHRAF: Yeah, I'm not so good on this, so what I'm going to do is, I'm going to bring in the horse.

ASHRAF WALKS THROUGH A DOOR BEHIND THE COUNTER, THEN RE-EMERGES A MOMENT LATER LEADING A PERFECTLY NORMAL HORSE. THE CUSTOMER IS QUIETLY AMAZED.

ASHRAF: Okay, I'm just gonna tell the horse what the problem is.

THE BEMUSED CUSTOMER WATCHES AS ASHRAF CLOSES HIS EYES AND NUZZLES THE HORSE MYSTICALLY, BREATHING ITS SCENT. HE IS HORSE-WHISPERING. AFTER A WHILE, ASHRAF COMES OUT OF HIS REVERIE AND TALKS NORMALLY TO THE CUSTOMER.

ASHRAF: The horse says – did you disable the antivirus software before you done the installation?

CUSTOMER: Um. No I didn't.

ASHRAF RETURNS TO HORSE WHISPERING, RUNNING HIS HANDS OVER THE BEAST'S FLANKS.

ASHRAF: (WHISPERS) Talk to me... Give me your wisdom...

THE HORSE JUST STANDS THERE. ASHRAF SNAPS OUT OF IT AGAIN.

Eh Sanjay, geezer
ask a horse about
a iPod, innit!

ASHRAF: The horse says you need to press F2, which take you into set-up. Then you disable the antivirus software, install XP, and it should run fine.

CUSTOMER: Great. Thank you.

ASHRAF: Yeah. It's a good horse, this one. One of the best we've had.

CUSTOMER: Actually, I've got a problem with my iPod.

CUSTOMER PULLS OUT AN IPOD. ASHRAF NUZZLES THE HORSE, JUST FOR A MOMENT.

ASHRAF: The horse says it doesn't know anything about iPods.

CUSTOMER: (DISAPPOINTED) Oh.

ASHRAF: Come on, boss. It's just a horse.

THE CUSTOMER EXITS.

ASHRAF: (TO HIS COLLEAGUE) Eh Sanjay, geezer ask a horse about a iPod, innit!

I'd love to get myself a job but I can't.

Why not?

I am a gay.

DAFYDD — MUM

INT: KITCHEN.

TOM V/O: This young man is what we call a homosexual. Some people in Britain are heterosexual. I myself am bisexual. Well, at my time of my life, I can't afford to be too picky.

DAFYDD IS SAT IN PVC PYJAMAS AT THE TABLE, CUTTING OUT PICTURES OF WILL YOUNG FROM MAGAZINES AND STICKING THEM INTO A SCRAPBOOK.

DAFYDD: (SINGS) 'I think I'm gonna leave right now, before I falls any deeper. I think I'm gonna leave right now, for I am feeling weaker and weaker.'

MUM ENTERS, WITH LOTS OF SHOPPING BAGS.

MUM: Can you give me a hand with the shopping, Dafydd?

DAFYDD: Oh, I would do, Ma, but I'm a little busy at the moment. I'm updating my Will Young scrapbook.

MUM: Oh right.

MUM DISAPPOINTEDLY STARTS TO UNPACK THE SHOPPING.

DAFYDD: He's been such an inspiration to me, as the only gay in the village – so brave the way he came out as gay just after he won *Pop Idol*.

MUM: Yes.

DAFYDD: Did you remember my Smarties?

SHE REACHES INTO ONE OF THE BAGS AND HANDS THEM OVER.

MUM: There you go. (SENSITIVELY) Now, me and your da have been talking and we're thinking it was time maybe you got yourself a job.

DAFYDD: I'd love to get myself a job but I can't.

MUM: Why not?

DAFYDD: I am a gay.

MUM: Oh rubbish.

DAFYDD: There's loads of jobs I'd love to do but can't because of my sexuality.

MUM: Like what?

DAFYDD: Hairdresser. Airline Steward. Children's TV presenter. But they simply don't employ the gays.

MUM: Of course they do. (ENCOURAGING) And... if you got yourself a job you could rent your own flat.

DAFYDD: (INCREDULOUS) How can I rent a flat? I'm a gay. Oh I can just see it now. 'Hello landlord. I like mens' bottoms.' How's that gonna go down?!

MUM: Couldn't you at least sign on? Then we'd have a bit of money coming in.

DAFYDD: I can't go down the job centre.

MUM: (SARCASTIC) Why? Because you're gay?

DAFYDD: (WITH INCREASING ANGER) That's right. I'm a homo. I'm a bender. I'm a fairy. I'm a poofter. (THROUGH CROCODILE TEARS) Ma, I'm a bumboy!

DAFYDD BREAKS DOWN.

MUM: I know.

DAFYDD: (IMMEDIATELY SNAPPING OUT OF IT) Oh sorry. I didn't think I'd mentioned it.

MUM: Well, make yourself useful, and help me put the shopping away.

DAFYDD: Mother, I am at a critical moment with my Pritt Stick.

MUM: Dafydd.

DAFYDD SIGHS, FEEBLY ATTEMPTS TO PICK UP A BAG AND IMMEDIATELY PUTS IT DOWN AGAIN.

DAFYDD: Oh I can't lift it. I'm gay.

MUM: Give it here, you big poof!

DAFYDD: Homophobe!

MUM: Oh don't be stupid!

DAFYDD: I'm reporting you to Childline!

DAFYDD HEADS FOR THE DOOR.

MUM: What?

DAFYDD: (EMOTIONAL) My own mother rejects me, simply for the crime of wanting mens' todgers in my bumbum. Good day!

DAFYDD EXITS DRAMATICALLY.

SID/NEIGHBOUR WATCH — LLOYD

EXT: LARCHWOOD CLOSE.

TOM V/O: In Grumble, just north of Little Moan, lies the home of local Neighbour Watch group leader, Sid Pegg.

SID PEGG RAISES A UNION FLAG UP A POLE IN HIS FRONT GARDEN. AS HE FINISHES, HE SOLEMNLY SALUTES THE FLAG.

INT: SID'S SUBURBAN HOUSE/LIVING ROOM. AS BEFORE, A FEW NEIGHBOURS ARE SAT AS SID TALKS. AMONG THEM ARE GILLIAN, A MIDDLE-AGED VICAR; DEAN AND HIS PREGNANT PARTNER CAROLINE, AND LLOYD SNOW. MEANWHILE SID PEGG, IS ADDRESSING THE ROOM.

SID: Okay. Welcome to tonight's meeting of Neighbour Watch. Now, did anyone witness the events of Sunday afternoon?

GROUP: No, no I didn't etc.

SID: Fifteen hundred hours approx. Imately. An empty can of Lilt was kicked down the close by a gang of yob.

GILLIAN: Is that all?

SID: If only it was, Mrs Vicar. On Monday – less than twenty-four hours after the Lilt incident – some mindless thug defaced the Larchwood Close road sign. They put two dots in the 'o's to make it look like a pair of titties.

THE GROUP LAUGH.

SID: There is nothing funny about a pair of woman's titties. Titties are beautiful. They are, in fact, my favourite part of a lady. Apart from the general fanny area.

WOMAN: (OOV) Shall I put your turkey burgers on?

SID: Yes, wife. Turkeys burgers – go! (TO HIMSELF) Right, where was I? Titties. Fanny. Turkey burgers. (TO GROUP) Ah yes, self-defence. Sometimes it is necessary to arm ourselves. Which is why I always sleep with this under my pillow –

There is nothing funny about a pair of woman's titties. Titties are beautiful. They are, in fact, my favourite part of a lady. Apart from the general fanny area.

PRODUCES A PILLOW.

SID: – another pillow! To smother them. (RAISES FIST) Britain fights back. (TO DEAN) You two married yet?

DEAN: No.

SID: Shame for the kid. It will be a bastard. (TO ALL) Right, can I have a volunteer, please?

NO HANDS GO UP. SID POINTS AT LLOYD.

SID: Lloyd. I saw your hand go up. Alright little fella. Little Lloyd Snow. Number seven. He rents – he doesn't own.

LLOYD RELUCTANTLY GETS UP.

SID: (TO GROUP) I don't know if you know – Lloyd was actually a contestant on *The Weakest Link*.

GILLIAN: Oh yes, I saw you on it.

SID: Sorry. If people are gonna start shouting things out, there's just gonna be chaos. (CALLS) Wife?

WOMAN: (OOV) Yes?

SID: Bird's Eye Potato Waffles – go! (TO LLOYD) Right, what do we do if one of these bastards – (TO DEAN AND CAROLINE) Sorry – (TO ALL) attacks you in your home? (TO LLOYD) Now Lloyd, you're gonna get me in a headlock and I'm gonna get out of it. Whatever I say, whatever I do, don't let go, okay? Right. Go.

LLOYD AWKWARDLY PUTS SID IN A HEADLOCK.

SID: Tighter. Tighter.

LLOYD DOES SO.

SID: That's nothing. Tighter.

SID TRIES FOR QUITE A WHILE TO GET OUT OF THE HEADLOCK BUT FAILS.

SID: Alright Lloyd, that's enough! (BARELY AUDIBLE) Please. I beg you. Let go.

LLOYD RELEASES SID, WHOSE HAIR AND CLOTHES ARE RUFFLED. SID RUBS HIS SORE NECK.

SID: And that's how you get out of a headlock. You just say that you've had enough and then they should let go. Thank you Lloyd. Thank you very much.

AS LLOYD GOES TO SIT BACK DOWN SID SLAPS HIM ON THE BACK OF THE HEAD.

SID: (CALLS) Wife. Alphabetti Spaghetti. Go!

MR MANN – ROY'S FANCY DRESS

INT: ROY'S FANCY DRESS SHOP. MR MANN ENTERS EATING A BAG OF CRISPS. HE THROWS THE BAG TO THE FLOOR AND WIPES HIS HANDS ON SOME OF THE HANGING CLOTHES.

TOM V/O: Business is brisk at this fancy dress shop. Fancy Dress Parties were invented in 1971 by Professor Ian Fancy Dress Party.

ROY: Right, well, what can I do for you?

MR MANN: If you wouldn't mind.

ROY: Right.

MR MANN: I have been invited to a fancy dress party and want to go as the comedian David Baddiel.

ROY: David Baddiel?

MR MANN: Yes. *Unplanned* era, please. Not *The Mary Whitehouse Experience*.

ROY: You are being a little specific.

MR MANN: I want to go as the author and humorist David Baddiel.

ROY: Oh dear. (CALLS) Margaret? Margaret?

LONG PAUSE. THE PAIR EXCHANGE SMILES.

MARGARET: Yes?

ROY: There's a gentleman here wants to know if we've got any David Baddiel costumes.

MARGARET: I don't think so. No.

ROY: She says she doesn't think so. No.

MR MANN: Oh.

I want to go as the author and humorist David Baddiel.

ROY: Oh.

MARGARET: We've got a Punt and Dennis but I think the Punt's out.

ROY: She says we've got a Punt and Dennis but she thinks the Punt's out.

MR MANN: No.

ROY: (CALLS) No.

MARGARET: Ooh, we've got a Statto outfit.

ROY: She says ooh, we've got a Statto outfit.

MR MANN: No. I only really like David.

ROY: I don't know what to suggest.

MR MANN: I'm in no hurry.

ROY: Well, I tell you what. Why don't I try to fashion a David Baddiel outfit out of some the more nondescript items we have in the shop?

MR MANN: That would be most kind.

ROY: Right, if you'd like to wait in our changing room over here.

ROY USHERS MR MANN OVER TO THE CHANGING ROOM AND DRAWS THE CURTAIN. ROY GRABS A COUPLE OF ITEMS OF CLOTHING.

ROY: (TO HIMSELF) Right. If I give you Rory McGrath's jumper, Martin Clunes' chinos and Sanjeev Bhaskar's espadrilles. And Terry Waites' beard.

ROY PASSES THE ITEMS THROUGH THE CURTAIN.

ROY: Well, how are you getting on?

THE CURTAINS OPEN AND WE SEE THE REAL DAVID BADDIEL.

DAVID: (OVERDUBBED BY MR MANN) Nothing like him.

ROY: No.

DAVID BADDIEL WITHDRAWS AND MR MANN IMMEDIATELY REAPPEARS THROUGH THE CURTAIN.

MR MANN: Thank you very much.

EPISODE

LOU AND ANDY — RUGBY

EXT: RUGBY STADIUM.

TOM V/O: Rugby is very popular in Britain, as it allows men to act out sado-masochistic homoerotic fantasies in the safety of a sporting context.

A LOCAL RUGBY MATCH IS TAKING PLACE. LOU AND ANDY ARE IN THE DISABLED ENCLOSURE.

LOU: Oh dear. Look's like Herby Town are gonna lose again.

ANDY: Yeah, I know.

LOU: You said it yourself. The team are strong on power but lack the delicate agility and finesse to ultimately fulfill their potential.

ANDY: Yeah, they're crap.

Oh dear. Look's like Herby Town are gonna lose again.

You said it yourself. The team are strong on power but lack the delicate agility and finesse to ultimately fulfill their potential.
Yeah, they're crap.

LOU: Oh well. I'm gonna get meself a tin of pop. Do you want one?

ANDY: No, I'll just have yours.

LOU: Right.

LOU EXITS UP SOME STEPS. ON THE PITCH SOME HERBY TOWN PLAYERS ARE RUNNING IN A LINE, PASSING THE BALL ALONG. ANDY IS SUDDENLY ON THE PITCH, IN THE LINE, AND INTERCEPTS THE BALL. HE RUNS TOWARDS THE END OF THE PITCH AND SCORES A TRY. HE RUNS TRIUMPHANTLY TOWARDS THE CROWD, WHO CHEER, AND RETURNS TO HIS SEAT. LOU APPEARS WITH A CAN OF DRINK.

LOU: Did I miss anything?

ANDY: No. Boring.

LOU OPENS THE CAN AND ANDY TAKES IT FROM HIM.

EPISODE

SEBASTIAN AND MICHAEL — ARAB/ISRAELI CONFLICT

EXT: NO. 10 DOWNING STREET. A POLICEMAN STANDS GUARD. SEBASTIAN OPENS A CAR DOOR. THE PM AND HIS WIFE GET OUT OF THE CAR AND APPROACH THE FRONT DOOR OF THE HOUSE. THEY POSE FOR PHOTOS. SEBASTIAN STANDS IN FRONT OF SARAH, OBSCURING HER, SO THE PHOTOS BECOME ABOUT HIM AND THE PM.

TOM V/O: Meanwhile, the Prime Minister is returning from Parliament, which was opened today by Her Majesty the Queen. Though for an extra forty quid they could have had Kerry McFadden.

INT. DAY. PM'S OFFICE. MICHAEL AND GREGORY ARE SAT TOGETHER ON THE SOFA.

GREGORY: Prime Minister, here's a summary of the Arab-Israeli conflict.

GREGORY HANDS MICHAEL SOME PAPERS.

MICHAEL: Thank you.

MICHAEL: Do you have a copy of the draft treaty there?

GREGORY: That'll be in the Foreign Secretary's office. I'll just go and get that for you.

MICHAEL: Would you.

GREGORY GETS UP AND OPENS THE DOOR. SEBASTIAN IS DISCOVERED CROUCHING DOWN IN THE DOORWAY, AS IF HE WAS SPYING THROUGH THE KEYHOLE. HE REMAINS BENT OVER, AT GREGORY'S CROTCH. MEANWHILE, MICHAEL READS HIS NOTES.

GREGORY: Sebastian.

SEBASTIAN: Hello, Gregory.

GREGORY: Were you just spying on us through the keyhole?

SEBASTIAN: No, I was just checking out a faulty knob.

GREGORY: (WEARILY) Really?

STILL ON HIS KNEES, SEBASTIAN WAVES PAST GREGORY.

SEBASTIAN: Hi, Prime Minister.

MICHAEL: Hello, Sebastian.

GREGORY DOESN'T MOVE. SEBASTIAN MANAGES TO SQUEEZE PAST HIM.

GREGORY: I won't be a moment, Prime Minister.

GREGORY GIVES SEBASTIAN A LOOK BEFORE EXITING. SEBASTIAN SLUMPS DOWN ON THE SOFA VERY CLOSE TO MICHAEL, WHO IS STILL READING HIS PAPERS.

SEBASTIAN: So you're still taking him to the peace talks?

MICHAEL: Could you move down a bit?

SEBASTIAN: Of course.

SEBASTIAN MOVES SLIGHTLY CLOSER TO MICHAEL AND PUTS HIS ARM AROUND HIM.

MICHAEL: Yes, he's very up on foreign diplomacy.

SEBASTIAN: I can do that. I'm up on the foreign dip– thing.

MICHAEL: This is very complex. It's the Arab-Israeli conflict. It's about reaching an agreement over the Gaza Strip.

SEBASTIAN: I've got an idea. How about the Israelis 'ave it Monday to Friday and the other lot 'ave it weekends?

MICHAEL: I don't think that's going to work.

SEBASTIAN: Oooh. A *Trisha* special?

MICHAEL: I don't think so.

SEBASTIAN: No, it's on Channel Five now, ain't it? It's gone right off. Musical chairs!

GREGORY: How ridiculous.

WE REALISE THAT GREGORY – DOCUMENT IN HAND – HAS BEEN STANDING IN THE DOORWAY, LISTENING, FOR A WHILE.

SEBASTIAN: (UNDER BREATH BUT LOUDLY) Ooh. She's getting nasty. Hm. (TO GREGORY) Maybe I should just leave. Yeah, you're the one who should go to Israel with him because you are so up on the Arab-Israeli conflict and you are so plainly in love with him – oh dear, I've said it!

EPISODE

No, I was just checking out a faulty knob

MICHAEL: Sebastian, please!

SEBASTIAN: I hope you two have a great time!

GREGORY: You're embarrassing yourself!

SEBASTIAN: He doesn't love you. He's just using you for sex!

SEBASTIAN RUNS OUT, SLAMMING THE DOOR.

GREGORY: Unbelievable.

MICHAEL: I know.

GREGORY: Where were we?

GREGORY SITS DOWN NEXT TO MICHAEL. THEY START LOOKING AT THEIR PAPERS AGAIN.

MICHAEL: I'd like to make an amendment to page four, paragraph two. I don't think the Israelis are gonna go for that.

GREGORY: Yes, yes. Of course, Prime Minister.

MICHAEL: I do love you, Gregory.

THE PAIR LOOK INTO EACH OTHER'S EYES.

GREGORY: I know, Prime Minister.

THEY KISS TENDERLY.

Where were we?

EMILY AND FLORENCE – BABY

EXT: SEAFRONT.

TOM V/O: Have you ever tried cross-dressing? I did once, for thirty years, but it wasn't really for me.

A PROUD EMILY PUSHES AN OLD-FASHIONED HOODED PRAM ALONG. SHE WAVES AT PASSERS-BY.

EMILY: Morning, ha ha! Just a lady out with her baby, that is all.

Just a lady out with her baby that is all.

EPISODE

THERE ARE A FEW MOTHERS WITH KIDS. ONE IS SAT ON A BENCH DRINKING COFFEE. SHE IS WATCHING A NEARBY FIVE-YEAR-OLD GIRL PLAYING. EMILY APPEARS WITH HER PRAM.

MOTHER: (CALLS) Don't go too far, Jessica!

JESSICA: Okay, Mummy.

EMILY: Good afternoon. Not easy being a young mother, is it?

MOTHER: (A LITTLE UNCONVINCED) No, no. It isn't.

EMILY: How old are yours?

MOTHER: Jessica's five and Elliot's six months. And yours?

EMILY: Oh um... gave birth today. Just a few hours old really. Very little baby. Would you like to see her?

MOTHER: Okay. Yeah.

THE MOTHER GETS UP TO TAKE A LOOK.

MOTHER: Hello.

SHE IS QUITE STARTLED. TO SEE THAT THE BABY IS, IN FACT, FLORENCE, DONE UP IN A LITTLE BABY'S BONNET.

FLORENCE: Hello.

EMILY: Isn't she beautiful?

MOTHER: Y-yes. She's really quite something.

EMILY: Hark at us! (THEY SIT) Two young mothers. Let's talk about being pregnant and babies and... shit.

THE MOTHER RELUCTANTLY SITS BACK DOWN. HER BABY STARTS TO CRY A LITTLE.

MOTHER: Excuse me, I just need to feed mine.

Isn't she beautiful?

EMILY: Oh, and me.

THE MOTHER REACHES INTO HER BAG AND PULLS OUT A BABY BOTTLE WITH SOME MILK IN IT. EMILY RIFLES THROUGH HER HANDBAG AND PULLS OUT A CAN OF TENNENT'S EXTRA. SHE PASSES IT TO FLORENCE, WHO OPENS IT AND GULPS IT DOWN.

EMILY: These men – they don't know what we go through, do they? What with the long bit of time when it's in your tumtum and then when it comes out of your loolee. I have a loolee. I am a lady. A lady's loolee.

THE MOTHER LOOKS BEMUSED. FLORENCE LETS RIPS WITH A LOUD, LOW BURP.

FLORENCE: Got any of them scotch eggs?

JESSICA: (OOV) Okay, Mummy!

EMILY: (SOTTO, TO FLORENCE) Will you please do this properly, Baby Flo?!

FLORENCE: When's it my turn to push the pram?

EMILY: Ssssh!

JESSICA RUNS OVER AND SPOTS EMILY.

JESSICA: Mummy, why is that man wearing a dress? And why is the fat man with a moustache dressed as a baby?

WE REVEAL AN EXASPERATED FLORENCE READING A COPY OF *AUTOTRADER*.

FLORENCE: (MAN'S VOICE) I've had enough of this!

FLORENCE CLAMBERS OUT OF THE PRAM.

EMILY: Please, please, baby Flo.

FLORENCE: (MAN'S VOICE) Right, I've had enough of this. Forget it!

FLORENCE STORMS OFF. WE SEE HIS NAPPY AND LITTLE BOOTEES.

EMILY: (EMBARRASSED) They grow up so quickly these days.

EMILY GETS UP AND PUSHES THE PRAM AFTER BABY FLO.

EMILY: Little Flo...? Little Flo...?

TOM V/O: If you have been affected by any of the issues raised in tonight's programme you may like to know that a special helpline has been set up. I think it's '0' something and then some other numbers – there may be a '7' in there somewhere, if that's any help. Good try.

Mummy, why is that man wearing a dress? And why is the fat man with a moustache dressed as a baby?

The Daily T

SIC
ST
FA
OUR

BRITAIN'S BEST-SELLING

www.telegraph.co.uk

Sir Norman resignation 'inevitable'

Future looks bleak for Sir Norman

By Paul Hardon
Political Noseyparker

SENIOR government sources hinted last night that Sir Norman Fry will almost certainly have to resign his position in the cabinet after further revelations yesterday in a tabloid newspaper. The Prime Minister was quick to distance himself from the troubled father-of-two at a trade union meeting yesterday, calling Fry's latest scandal 'regrettable'. In response to increasing calls for him to quit, Sir Norman called a 3pm press conference at his Berkshire home and read the following statement.

'On Tuesday night, after a late-night session at the House of Commons, I decided to take a stroll. On Hampstead Heath. Whilst there I met a young blond-haired man who had lost his dog. I offered to go into the

Finally the end for Sir Norman?
Have we finally seen the end of an eventful political career for Sir Norman Fry? A Commons insider revealed, 'We had all seen it coming.' Some say that the latest string of events has been engineered by people who want to see the back of Sir Norman.

No 10: It's a messy job but someone's got to do it.
News: Page 4

Is there any more Fish to Fry?
Editorial Comment: Page 17

look for it. Unfortunately the animal in question was nowhere to be seen so I gave him fifty pounds so that he could buy another one. At that point my clothes accidentally fell off. Soon after I lost my footing and slipped on a wet blade of grass. As I fell, I accidentally pulled down the young

man's trousers and pants.
In the melee I reached out and grabbed what I thought was a branch. In order to help myself up. I repeatedly tugged on it, until my face was covered in what I assumed was sap. At this point the police arrived and I can see now how this whole series of events could have been misconstrued.

Despite a slew of recent allegations – some of which are too distasteful to be reported in a family newspaper – Fry's wife Pippa was said to be standing by her husband. A friend of the couple said, 'Pippa has always been unlucky in love.'

Before marrying Sir Norman she is said to have dated Michael Portillo at university, had a relationship with Liberal MP Mark Oaten and was briefly engaged to Peter Tatchell.

Continued on pages 4 & 5

Sir Norma

NEWSPAPER OF THE DECADE

elegraph

NG STOMACH
NG SCAM OF UK's
HTERS

ER REPORTER'S FULL STORY PAGE 12

Monday, September 8, 2006   No 46,940   65p

AILY

ife Pippa yesterday, 'we must carry on with our lives.'

POSTAGE PAID
HQ 34

EPISODE *six*

TOM V/O: Britain, Britain, Britain. The land that gave the world so much. Mad cow disease, happy slapping and Sky One's *Dream Team*. But who are what live here, sir? Come with me, as we meet the inhabitants of Little Britain. Do you really like it? Is it is it wicked? We're lovin' it, lovin' it, lovin' it. We're lovin' it like that!

VICKY POLLARD – LOTTERY

INT: NEWSAGENT SHOP.

TOM V/O: This is Vicky Pollard. She is one of Britain's most beautiful women.

VICKY APPROACHES THE COUNTER.

VICKY: Are you the newsasian?

SHOPKEEPER: Yeah.

VICKY: Do you like do the lottery or summin' or nuffin'?

SHOPKEEPER: (INDICATES SIGN) Yeah. You can buy your ticket here.

VICKY WAVES A LOTTERY TICKET.

VICKY: No I don't need to 'cause I actually like won the whole jackpot and that.

SHOPKEEPER: Really?

VICKY: Yeah I got my ticket right here.

VICKY HANDS OVER THE TICKET. THE SHOPKEEPER STUDIES IT.

VICKY: Oh yeah and it was a Saturday one not a Wednesday one cause the money's well nothing on a Wednesday it's like only a million quid. It's well not worth the stress. Oh yeah, and I definitely won it and if Coleen McGovern says I'm lying then don't listen to her 'cause she's got one of them nut allergies 'cause one time we was all round the back of Nandos and I gave her a peanut Revel only I told her it was a coffee one and she ate it and she had to go to hospital and she nearly died and she well blamed me for it and I'm like 'it's not my fault you're so gay you can't even eat a peanut'.

THE SHOPKEEPER HANDS BACK THE TICKET.

SHOPKEEPER: You made this yourself.

VICKY: No but yeah but no but yeah but no but yeah but no but yeah but no but yeah but no but...

DURING THIS A CUSTOMER ENTERS.

CUSTOMER: Twenty Bensons, please.

THE SHOPKEEPER SERVES HIM. VICKY NODS AT HIM.

VICKY: ...yeah but I did but I didn't but I did but I didn't because I couldn't because I was actually busy doing two million hours community service and anyway I couldn't have made it myself even if I had actually wanted to actually because I can't read or write because I'm like totally lexdykslyk.

SHOPKEEPER: Stop wasting my time.

VICKY: Oh my God I so can't believe you just said that. You actually owe me fifty billion pounds or summin' or nuffin'.

SHOPKEEPER: Your ticket is not valid.

VICKY: All right. Ten million quid and a bag of Discos.

SHOPKEEPER: Out.

VICKY: Five hundred quid and a Kinder Surprise.

SHOPKEEPER: Go.

yeahbutIdidbutIdidn'tbutIdidbutIdidn'tbecause

Icouldn'tbecauseIwasactuallybusydoingtwomillion

hourscommunityserviceandanywayIcouldn'thave

madeitmyselfevenifIhadactuallywantedtoactually

becauseIcan'treadorwritebecauseI'mliketotally

lexdykslyk.

VICKY: Four pack of Breezers.

SHOPKEEPER: No.

VICKY: Chomp.

SHOPKEEPER: No.

VICKY: Bag of Skips and I'll give you a gobjob.

SHOPKEEPER POINTS TO THE DOOR.

VICKY: You've like so lost a good customer. I am always in here robbin'.

SHE HEADS FOR THE DOOR, GRABS A COPY OF *ANGLING TIMES*, WALKS OUT, WAVES IT PROVOCATIVELY AT THE SHOP-KEEPER, THEN THROWS IT OVER HER SHOULDER.

VICKY: I don't even want it.

BUBBLES DEVERE – DEPARTURE

TOM V/O: Over at Hill Grange, former mistress of Prince Philip, Bubbles DeVere, is undergoing some acupuncture.

INT: HILL GRANGE HEALTH SPA/TREATMENT ROOM. BUBBLES IS LYING FACE DOWN COVERED BY A TOWEL. GITA IS PUTTING SOME ACUPUNCTURE NEEDLES INTO HER.

BUBBLES: And I tell you, Gita, darling, I can't wait to see the back of both of them.

GITA: Just as well, Miss Bubble, because I just saw them leaving.

BUBBLES: What?!

INT: HILL GRANGE HEALTH SPA/RECEPTION. VARIOUS STAFF ARE MILLING ABOUT. ROMAN AND DESIREE APPROACH RECEPTION. DESIREE IS COMPLAINING UNDER HER BREATH. ROMAN GOES TO PAY THE BILL.

ROMAN: If we could have the luggage in the Merc, please.

MANAGERESS: I see you're leaving us early, Mr DeVere.

ROMAN: Yeah, I'm afraid so.

DESIREE: Yes, that bitch has ruined our honeymoon!

ROMAN: Darling, please don't make a scene.

DESIREE: I'll make a scene if I want to, baby!

BUBBLES: You didn't even come to say goodbye.

BUBBLES IS STANDING, NAKED, AT THE TOP OF THE STAIRS. HER ENTIRE BODY IS COVERED IN ACUPUNCTURE NEEDLES. SHE RESEMBLES A PORCUPINE.

ROMAN: I was going to but I thought it was better if we just slipped away.

BUBBLES: I see. (SHE DESCENDS) Goodbye then, Roman.

ROMAN: Goodbye Bubbles.

ROMAN AND DESIREE TURN TO LEAVE. BUBBLES STRETCHES HER ARMS OUT.

BUBBLES: Hold me, Roman. One last time!

ROMAN LOOKS BUBBLES UP AND DOWN.

ROMAN: I can't.

BUBBLES: Why not, darling?

ROMAN: Because you're covered in needles.

BUBBLES: But Roman...

ROMAN LEAVES.

DESIREE: (TO BUBBLES) He's staying with me, baby. He's mine, all mine!

DESIREE LAUGHS IN FITS AND STARTS. SHE GOES TO LEAVE THEN RETURNS FOR ONE LAST LAUGH BEFORE LEAVING AGAIN. A BEATEN BUBBLES IS LEFT ON THE STAIRS, WEEPING.

I'll make a scene if I want to, baby!

CAROL – COMPUTER SAYS YES

EXT. DAY. SUNSEARCHERS TRAVEL AGENTS. WE SEE CAROL BEER INSIDE THE SHOP, STANDING AT THE WINDOW. SHE PINS UP A POSTER THAT READS 'KUWAIT – SELF-CATERING – £209'.

TOM V/O: Britain can proudly boast the dirtiest beaches, the most disappointing views and some of the flattest hills in the world. Still, some Britons choose to book holidays abroad.

INT: TRAVEL AGENTS. CAROL BEER IS SAT AT HER DESK. AN OLD MAN IS IN FRONT OF HER.

OLD MAN: I'd like a round the world cruise, please, leaving in March, returning September, travelling first class, for about seven hundred pounds?

CAROL HAS A LOOK THAT SAYS 'YOU HAVE GOT TO BE KIDDING'. SHE TYPES IN A FEW KEYS.

CAROL: (AMAZED) Computer says yes. Carol looks disgruntled.

THE OLD MAN COUGHS IN HER FACE.

LOU AND ANDY —
MRS MEAD 1

INT: ANDY'S FLAT.

TOM V/O: Meanwhile in Herby, Lou has something upsetting to tell Andy.

ANDY IS IN HIS PYJAMAS WATCHING *BALAMORY* AND SINGING ALONG. HE HAS AN ENORMOUS AMOUNT OF BUTTER NEXT TO HIS TOAST. LOU APPEARS. HE SEEMS SUBDUED. ANDY SINGS ALONG TO THE THEME TUNE.

ANDY: 'What's the story in Balamory? Wouldn't you like to know? What's the story in Balamory? Where would you like to go?'

LOU: How's your toast?

ANDY: Too buttery.

LOU CROUCHES DOWN IN FRONT OF ANDY.

LOU: Now, you remember I told you my mum was very ill.

ANDY: Yeah, I know.

LOU: Well, I'm sorry to say that she passed off during the night.

ANDY: Can't see the telly.

ANDY USHERS LOU OUT OF THE WAY.

LOU: Oh sorry. So I'm gonna have to go back to the Isle of Wight for a few days to look after my dad and sort out all the funeral arrangements.

ANDY: So selfish. What about me?

LOU: Well, I've spoken to Social Services and arranged some temporary cover for the week.

ANDY: But I like it when you're here.

LOU: Oh, I'm sure the lady they'll be sending will be very nice.

THERE IS A SHARP RAPPING AT THE DOOR.

I don't like her...

LOU: Ooh she's early.

LOU EXITS.

LOU: (OOV) Hello. You must be Mrs Mead.

MRS MEAD: (OOV) Yes. Yes. I've no time for niceties. Where is he?

LOU: Just through here.

LOU ENTERS WITH MRS MEAD, A LOUD BRUSQUE IRISH LADY. SHE HANDS LOU HER COAT AND TAKES OFF HER HAT. SHE CARRIES A BAG WITH CLEANING GEAR IN IT. SHE ROLLS HER SLEEVES UP.

MRS MEAD: Good morning, Mr Pipkin.

LOU: Andy, this is Mrs Mead.

ANDY: I don't like her.

LOU: Now come on, Andy. Don't be rude.

MRS MEAD: I don't care whether he likes me or not.

LOU: Well, I better be off. Here are the keys, Mrs Mead. I'll call you in a few days. (TO ANDY) Bye, Andy.

ANDY: (BESEECHING) Don't go.

LOU EXITS, GUILTILY. MRS MEAD TURNS THE TELLY OFF.

MRS MEAD: This place is a pigsty. We're going to clear it up.

SHE WHEELS HIM OVER TO THE SHELVING UNIT ROUGHLY. SHE HANDS HIM A CLOTH.

MRS MEAD: You do the bottom shelf. I'll do the top.

ANDY SITS STILL, IN A STATE OF SHOCK.

MRS MEAD: Come on!

SHE TAPS HIS HAND THEN BEGINS CLEANING.

EPISODE

But together we fooled the world. Everywhere we went people were enchanted by our feminine charms and beauty and shit.

EMILY AND FLORENCE – FLORENCE WANTS OUT

INT: EMILY'S HOUSE.

TOM V/O: Next we visit Oldhaven where transvestite Emily Howard is relaxing at home with a book. I like to relax by saying cruel and hurtful things to my elderly mother.

EMILY LOOKS THROUGH AN ILLUSTRATED VICTORIAN-LOOKING PICTURE BOOK. ON THE PAGES ARE VARIOUS IMAGES OF KITTENS, PUPPIES, RABBITS ETC DRESSED IN VICTORIAN CLOTHES. AS SHE TURNS EACH PAGE SHE SIGHS WITH PLEASURE. THE DOORBELL RINGS.

EMILY: (CALLS) One moment, dear.

EMILY OPENS THE DOOR. THERE IS FRED (FLORENCE), OUT OF DRAG. IN THE BACKGROUND WE SEE A CAR WAITING, WITH MAUREEN IN THE DRIVER'S SEAT. EMILY'S FACE DROPS.

EMILY: Oh. Florence.

FRED: It's, er, Fred.

EMILY: What are you dressed as? You look most peculiar.

FRED: We need to talk.

EMILY: Oh. Come in, then.

FRED: Look, I can't stop. I just came to say goodbye, really.

EMILY: Goodbye?

FRED: The wife came home from the pub and found me trying on her wedding dress. She hit the roof. She says she's had enough.

EMILY: But together we fooled the world. Everywhere we went people were enchanted by our feminine charms and beauty and shit.

FRED: I dunno. You were always better at it than me, anyway.

EMILY: But –

FRED: Look, Maureen's in the car. I'd better go. Sorry.

FRED TURNS AWAY.

EMILY: One moment. I have something for you.

FRED TURNS BACK.

FRED: What is it?

EMILY: Un petit moment.

EMILY DISAPPEARS.

MAUREEN HONKS THE CAR HORN.

MAUREEN: Come on, Fred!

FRED: Won't be a minute, love.

EMILY RETURNS. SHE HOLDS UP A BEAUTIFUL-LOOKING DRESS.

FRED: Oh. It's silk?

EMILY: Yes, antique.

FRED: It's very nice but I couldn't possibly –

EMILY: (GRUFF MAN'S VOICE) You love it. You know you love it.

FLORENCE: Well, perhaps I (FLIPPING TO FULL 'LADY' MODE) could just try it on for a moment.

EMILY: (LADY VOICE) Come in, Florence my dear!

FLORENCE: Thank you, my lady friend.

FLORENCE DISAPPEARS INTO THE HOUSE. EMILY LEANS OUT.

EMILY: (CALLS) Maureen?

MAUREEN: Yes?

EMILY BLOWS A VERY UNLADYLIKE RASPBERRY AT MAUREEN, FLICKING V-SIGNS AND JUMPING UP AND DOWN TRIUMPHANTLY, BEFORE GOING BACK INSIDE AND SLAMMING THE DOOR SHUT.

LINDA – FATTY BUM BUM

INT: LINDA'S OFFICE.

TOM V/O: If you're a young person who wishes to eat only chili con carne for three years and then spend the rest of your life in debt, why not go to university?

LINDA SITS OPPOSITE ROLAND, A YOUNG FAT BLACK MAN.

ROLAND: And I just wanted to defer a year, because I've decided to run for Student Union President.

LINDA: Ooh, good luck. I think there's a form you'll need to fill in. Martin'll know.

LINDA PICKS UP THE PHONE AND DIALS.

LINDA: Martin, it's Linda. Is there a form you need to fill in if you want to defer a year? It's Roland Burrell. How can I describe him? Glasses. Colourful shirts. Not keen on salad. Think Eddie Murphy in *The Klumps*. Makes you want to say 'Ro-land. I only want to help you, Ro-land'. Would make a great Barry White on *Stars In Their Eyes*. That's right. Fatty Fatty Bum Bum.

ROLAND LOOKS SHOCKED.

'hey fatty bum bum, sweet sugar dumpling.'

LINDA: He says go straight up.

ROLAND: Thanks a lot.

ROLAND LEAVES. LINDA DOES SOME MARKING.

LINDA: (HUMS TO HERSELF) 'Hey fatty bum bum, sweet sugar dumpling.'

LOU AND ANDY — MRS MEAD 2

INT: ANDY'S FLAT. THE LIVING ROOM IS LOOKING TIDIER. MRS MEAD, SLEEVES ROLLED UP, IS POLISHING A BRASS CANDLESTICK HOLDER. ANDY IS SLOWLY POLISHING THE OTHER ONE. THERE IS NEWSPAPER ON THE FLOOR AND BRASSO.

MRS MEAD: Holy Mary Mother of God. Look at that. This candlestick holder's filthy. It looks like it's never been cleaned at all.

ANDY: Yeah, I know.

MRS MEAD: You've been in that there chair for many years, have you?

ANDY: Yeah.

MRS MEAD: (SIGHS) Oh the Lord works in mysterious ways. And you've no feeling in your legs whatsoever?

ANDY: (SHAKING HIS HEAD) No.

MRS MEAD: You can't feel this?

MRS MEAD HITS ANDY ON HIS KNEE WITH THE CANDLESTICK HOLDER.

ANDY: No.

MRS MEAD: What about this?

SHE HITS HIS LEGS HARDER.

ANDY: (WINCES) No.

MRS MEAD: Not even this?

SHE GIVES HIS LEG A REAL WHACK.

ANDY: (AFTER A PAUSE) No.

MRS MEAD: Oh you poor thing. Right, we need some more Brasso.

MRS. MEAD GETS UP, LEANING ON ANDY'S KNEE. SHE GOES INTO THE KITCHEN.

ANDY: Ow. Ooow. OOOOOW!

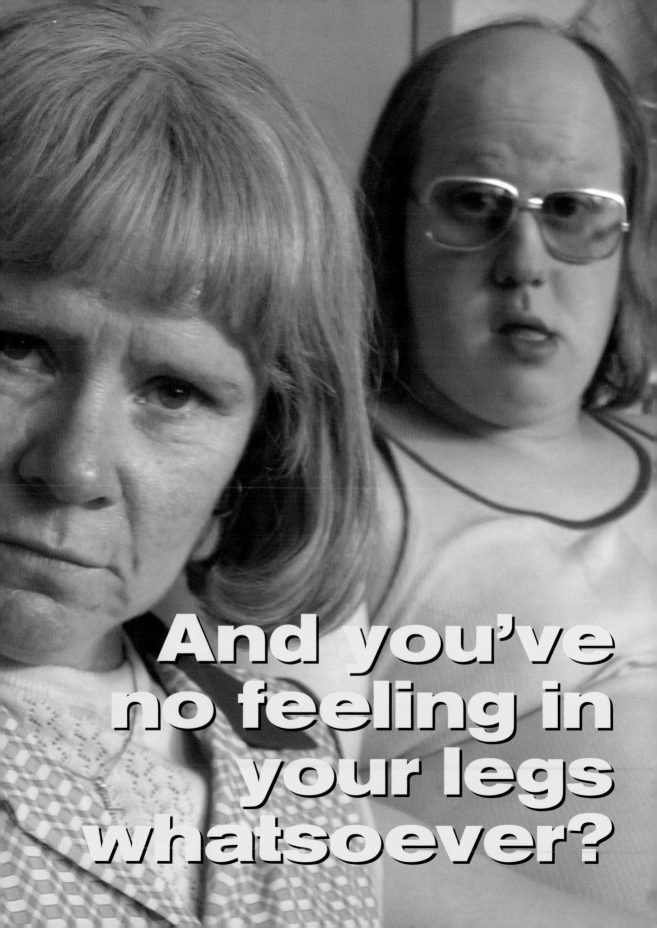

And you've no feeling in your legs whatsoever?

MRS EMERY – DOCTOR

INT: DOCTOR'S SURGERY.

TOM V/O: If you think you might become ill in six weeks' time then why not book an appointment with your local GP?

DOCTOR BOSTOCK: (ON INTERCOM) Carla, would you bring the next patient in please?

MRS EMERY ENTERS.

And it's just the knee that's... troubling you, is it?

DOCTOR BOSTOCK: Ah, Mrs Emery. Nice to see you again.

MRS EMERY: Hello Doctor. It's bitter out.

MRS EMERY SITS DOWN.

DOCTOR BOSTOCK: Yes. So, what seems to be the trouble?

MRS EMERY: I've got a bit of a problem, Doctor.

DOCTOR BOSTOCK: Yes?

MRS EMERY: It's my knee. It's a little bit sore.

DOCTOR BOSTOCK: Right, well, we'd better have a look at you, hadn't we. If you can stand up over here?

MRS EMERY STANDS UP. THE DOCTOR CROUCHES DOWN. MRS EMERY LIFTS UP HER SKIRT A LITTLE. THE DOCTOR LOOKS AT HER KNEE.

DOCTOR BOSTOCK: Right. Ah, yes, it does look a little swollen. Have you banged it at all?

MRS EMERY: Well...

MRS EMERY STARTS PISSING. THE DOCTOR REMAINS AT WAIST HEIGHT AND OBSERVES THE URINE FLOW IN SHOCK.

MRS EMERY: ...the other night I knelt down to unplug the television set and I must have put too much weight on my knee and I think I felt something go.

DOCTOR BOSTOCK: And it's just the knee that's... troubling you, is it?

MRS EMERY: Just the knee, Doctor.

DOCTOR BOSTOCK: If you can, er, just sit down for a moment.

MRS EMERY SPOTS A NICE PAINTING ON THE WALL. SHE WALKS OVER TO IT, STILL PISSING.

MRS EMERY: Oh, that's a nice painting. Is that a Turner?

DOCTOR BOSTOCK: Er, yes, yes. It is. Please...

DOCTOR BOSTOCK LEADS MRS EMERY BACK TO HER SEAT, SITS DOWN AND STARTS TO WRITE A PRESCRIPTION. MRS EMERY STOPS PISSING AS SHE SITS DOWN.

MRS EMERY: Ooh, chair's a bit damp.

DOCTOR BOSTOCK: Yes, well I'm going to give you fluoxydicyllin, which is an anti-inflammatory. If the swelling hasn't gone down within a week come back and see me again.

THE DOCTOR HANDS HER A PRESCRIPTION.

MRS EMERY: Thank you, Doctor.

MRS EMERY RISES AND HEADS FOR THE DOOR. ON THE WAY SHE STARTS PISSING AGAIN.

DOCTOR BOSTOCK: Mrs Emery, are you sure there's nothing else that's troubling you?

MRS EMERY: I can't think of anything.

THE WATER IS NOW GUSHING OUT MORE VIOLENTLY THAN EVER.

MRS EMERY: Bit of water retention but otherwise I'm fine. Cheerio.

MRS EMERY EXITS. THE DOCTOR SURVEYS THE MESS.

MARJORIE DAWES/FATFIGHTERS – THE APOLOGY

INT: FATFIGHTERS.

TOM V/O: No, this isn't a zoo. These are not elephants. They are, in fact, human beings...

THE GROUP IS GATHERED AS USUAL. TANYA IS BEING WEIGHED. SHE HAS LOST SOME WEIGHT. THE GROUP APPLAUD.

MARJORIE: Yeah, don't get carried away. She's still a monster. Off you pop.

TOM V/O: ...as we pay our final visit to FatFighters.

TANYA RETURNS TO HER SEAT.

MARJORIE: Pat.

PAT GETS UP AND MAKES HER WAY TOWARD THE SCALES.

MARJORIE: She's such a pretty face, hasn't she? In the middle, there.

PAT SHOOTS MARJORIE A LOOK. SHE STEPS ON THE SCALES.

MARJORIE: Oh, you've put on two pounds. Oh dear. Oh it's not easy, is it? Do you wanna somehow drag yourself back to your seat? You see, your problem is, Pat, you're a classic yo-yo dieter. You go up and down.

PAT SITS. MARJORIE WALKS OVER TO THE BOARD, PICKS UP A PEN AND DRAWS ACCORDINGLY.

MARJORIE: You see, you've got your good foods here – you've got your lettuce, your Ryvita, your dust, and over here, you've got your bad foods – your choclit, your crisps, your cake – ooh man she fat because she love de cake – and here's you, stuck in the middle, yo-yoing between the two.

MARJORIE STEPS BACK. WE SEE THAT SHE HAS DRAWN PAT AS A PIG.

PAT: Marjorie, you've drawn me as a pig.

MARJORIE: Oh sorry.

MARJORIE DRAWS SOME HAIR ON THE PIG.

PAT: Do you know what? I don't need this any more. I'm not losing weight. Every time I come you're horrible to me. I've had enough.

PAT STANDS UP AND HEADS FOR THE DOOR.

MARJORIE: Don't go.

PAT: Well, apologise. Say sorry then.

MARJORIE: Say what?

MEERA: Say sorry.

MARJORIE: What?

Marjorie, you've drawn me as a pig.

MEERA: Say sorry.

MARJORIE: No, I can't... Do it again.

MEERA: Say sorry.

MARJORIE: Do it again.

MEERA: Say sorry.

MARJORIE: Do it again.

MEERA: Say sorry!

PAUL: Just say sorry to her!

MARJORIE: (TO PAT) Oh, you want me to say 'sorry'. (TO MEERA) Why didn't you say that?

MEERA: I did.

MARJORIE: Do it again.

MEERA: I did.

MARJORIE: Do it again.

MEERA: I did.

MARJORIE: Do it again.

MEERA: I did.

MARJORIE: Do it again.

PAT: I'm waiting for an apology.

MARJORIE: (TO MEERA) I'll come back to you, my love.

PAT: I don't see why you can't just say sorry?

PAUL: Yeah, come on.

MARJORIE: I can. I can say sorry.

PAT: Well, go on then.

MARJORIE: I'm gonna say it any minute now.

PAUL: Well, say it.

MARJORIE: I'm about to.

PAT: Go on.

MARJORIE: (VERY QUICKLY, UNDER HER BREATH) Sorry.

EPISODE

PAT: I didn't hear that.

MARJORIE: Well, I said it, so...

PAUL: We didn't hear it either. Come on, let's go.

THE GROUP START TO LEAVE.

MARJORIE: No, no, no. I'm gonna say it. I'm gonna say it. I'm gonna say it. I'm gonna say it. I'm gonna say it.

MARJORIE APPROACHES PAT (AND GROUP) AND TAKES HER BY BOTH HANDS. SHE TAKES A DEEP BREATH.

MARJORIE: Pat. I... am very... sorry (SHOUTS, ALMOST INVOLUNTARILY) ...that you're so fat!

MARJORIE IMMEDIATELY REALISES WHAT SHE HAS DONE.

MARJORIE: Oh! It just came out!

PAUL: I'm not putting up with this.

THE GROUP START TO LEAVE, SPEAKING OVER EACH OTHER.

TANYA: You need help.

PAT: So rude.

MEERA: Don't worry. We're not coming back.

MARJORIE: Do it again.

MARJORIE IS ALONE. SHE SIGHS CALMLY.

MARJORIE: I need some noo members.

I need some noo members

LINDA — CONFRONTATION

INT: LINDA'S OFFICE. LINDA IS DUNKING A BISCUIT INTO A MUG
OF COFFEE. SHE TAKES A BITE.

TOM V/O: Back in her office, Linda is taking
a tea break.

LINDA: Mmmm. Lovely biscuit.

THERE IS A CONFIDENT KNOCK ON THE DOOR

LINDA: Come in.

THE DOOR OPENS AND TEN STUDENTS ENTER, INCLUDING
ALL OF THE STUDENTS LINDA HAS SEEN THIS TERM AND LAST,
TOGETHER WITH A MAN WITH LONG GINGER HAIR (ELLIOT).

LINDA: Hallo? What's all this about?

TOBY: We've come to complain.

LINDA: About what?

PAUL ROBERTS: About the way you talk about
us all.

KENNETH LAU: Yeah, it's really insulting.

LINDA: I don't know what you mean. What have I said?

I've got the whole cast of Fraggle Rock here; they're not happy...

KENNETH LAU: Ching Chong Chinaman.

ROLAND: Fatty fatty bum bum.

MOLLY: Molly the Mole.

STEVE: Ali Bongo.

ELLIOT: Mick Hucknall.

NINA: Magnum PI.

PAUL ROBERTS: Oompah Loompah.

JO HARDING: Big fat lesbian.

ROBIN: (SHOUTS) Baldy!

LINDA: Your point being?

ROLAND: The point is that we want to make an official complaint.

LINDA: Well, I'm shocked. Let's get Martin down here now and sort out this awful mess.

LINDA TAKES ANOTHER BITE OF HER BISCUIT THEN PICKS UP THE PHONE.

LINDA: Martin, it's Linda. I've got the whole cast of *Fraggle Rock* here; they're not happy...

WE SEE THE GROUP LOOKING SHOCKED.

LEONARD 2 – MR JEFFERIES

TOM V/O: Do you keep a used tissue up your sleeve? If so, you are an old person, and probably live in a home like this.

INT: OLD PEOPLE'S HOME/DINING ROOM. VARIOUS ELDERLY PEOPLE ARE EATING. WE CAN HEAR THE TELEVISION IN THE BACKGROUND. LEONARD ENTERS AND APPROACHES AN ELDERLY GENTLEMAN (MR JEFFERIES) WHO IS STRUGGLING WITH HIS FOOD.

LEONARD: Hello, Mr Jefferies. How are we today?

MR JEFFERIES: Oh, very good.

MR JEFFERIES SHRUGS. LEONARD STANDS BEHIND HIM.

LEONARD: You having trouble with that? Let me help you.

MR JEFFERIES NODS, HELPLESSLY, AS LEONARD CUTS UP THE FOOD AND STARTS TO EAT IT.

LEONARD: That's better.

MR JEFFERIES GOES TO TAKE A SIP OF HIS DRINK.

LEONARD: Oh, thank you.

LEONARD TAKES IT FROM HIM AND WASHES DOWN HIS FOOD.

You having trouble with that? Let me help you.

LOU AND ANDY — MRS MEAD 3

INT: ANDY'S FLAT/LIVING ROOM. ANDY SITS, GLOWERING AT HIS STEW. MRS MEAD COMES IN FROM THE KITCHEN.

MRS MEAD: You barely touched your stew. There's your pudding.

MRS MEAD PLONKS DOWN A PEAR.

ANDY: I'm not good with fruit.

MRS MEAD: It's good for you.

ANDY: Lou always lets me have a choc-ice.

MRS MEAD: Lou's not here, is he?

ANDY: And I'm allowed to watch *Des and Mel*.

MRS MEAD: There'll be no Des in this flat. And no Mel neither. Television rots the mind. We'll make our own entertainment. Two, three, four... (SINGS PROUDLY) 'Onward, Christian soldiers, marching as to war...'

ANDY: I don't like it.

MRS MEAD: 'With the cross of Jesus going on before.'

ANDY: (FLATLY) Please stop.

MRS MEAD: (STANDING) 'Christ, the royal Master, leads against the foe...'

ANDY: You're making me ears hurt now.

MRS MEAD: 'Forward into battle, See His banners go!' (SITTING) Now, let us pray.

ANDY: Oh God...

I'm not good

with fruit.

With my physique I'll be able to get myself a job as a gogo dancer.

DAFYDD — LEAVING FOR LONDON

EXT: VILLAGE.

TOM V/O: Now we return to Llandewi Breffi, and the local pub of bum-troubler Dafydd Thomas.

INT: SCARECROW AND MRS KING. MYFANWY IS BEHIND THE BAR. A FEW LOCALS ARE NURSING THEIR PINTS. DAFYDD ENTERS. HE HAS A SMALL BATTERED SUITCASE.

MYFANWY: Hello Dafydd, Bacardi and Coke?

DAFYDD: No thank you, Myfanwy. I've not stopped by for a drink. I've come to say goodbye.

MYFANWY: Oh yes?

DAFYDD: Yes, Myfanwy. I'm leaving the village. Forever.

MYFANWY: Forever?

DAFYDD: Llandewi Breffi is not the place for an out gay man. (TO DRINKERS) Yeah, I'm gay! Get over it!

MYFANWY: Well, where are you going?

DAFYDD: London. With my physique I'll be able to get myself a job as a gogo dancer.

MYFANWY: Well, where are you gonna stay?

DAFYDD: At the YMCA. Apparently you can have a good meal, you can get yourself clean and you can hang out with all the guys.

MYFANWY: Well good for you, Dafydd.

DAFYDD: (EXCITED) I'm gonna live the gay dream, Myfanwy. I'm gonna go to gay bars and drink gay drinks. I'm gonna ride gay buses. And if I get peckish, Myfanwy, I'll just open up a packet of gay biscuits.

MYFANWY: Gay biscuits?

DAFYDD: This is London, Myfanwy. Everything's gay.

MYFANWY: And you're sure it's what you really want?

DAFYDD: Oh Myfanwy, I've known I was gay since I was twenty-two. It's all I've ever dreamed of.

MYFANWY: Come on, then. I'll walk you to the station.

DAFYDD: Thank you, Myfanwy.

MYFANWY COMES OUT FROM BEHIND THE COUNTER. DAFYDD HANDS HER HIS SUITCASE. THEY HEAD FOR THE DOOR.

DAFYDD: Well, I'm going, everybody. Well done. You've won. A victory for the bigots. I wonder how many more beautiful young gay men will be driven away from this village by your scorn. Well, none. Obviously. Because I am the only one.

HE OPENS THE DOOR. MYFANWY FOLLOWS, STRUGGLING WITH THE CASE.

EXT: COUNTRY PATH/STATION. MYFANWY – WITH CASE – FOLLOWS DAFYDD.

MYFANWY: This case is quite heavy, Dafydd.

DAFYDD: It would be, yes, Myfanwy. But I'm gay, you see. I can't really carry heavy objects.

MYFANWY: No. Well, I'm gonna miss you but I guess you're doing the right thing. Just think, this time tomorrow you could be in a nightclub heaving with young men, like G-A-Y...

DAFYDD: Is that a gay club?

MYFANWY: Yes, I think so.

DAFYDD: Well, I don't think I'll be going out on the first night, Myfanwy.

MYFANWY: You've got to get out there, Dafydd. Have yourself a bit of todger.

DAFYDD: I don't think that's going to happen.

MYFANWY: Of course it is. There's loads of gay guys in London. You won't be the only gay in the village anymore.

DAFYDD: No?

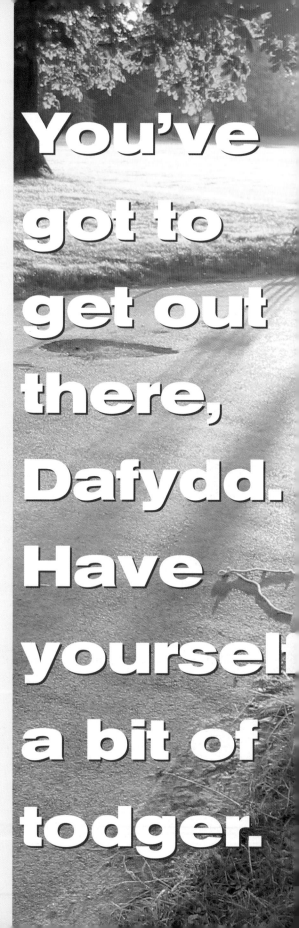

You've got to get out there, Dafydd. Have yourself a bit of todger.

MYFANWY: (CHEERFULLY) No. It'll be brilliant!

THEY ARRIVE AT THE STATION BARRIER. DAFYDD LOOKS UNCERTAIN.

MYFANWY: Right. Well. This is as far as I can go. Good luck, Dafydd.

SHE HANDS HIM HIS SUITCASE.

MYFANWY: Don't forget to write.

HE GIVES HER A PECK ON THE CHEEK.

DAFYDD: Goodbye, Myfanwy.

HE EXITS. WE STAY WITH MYFANWY, AS SHE GETS A BIT TEARY-EYED. SHE SEARCHES FOR HER HANDKERCHIEF. DAFYDD REAPPEARS.

DAFYDD: Doesn't look like I'm... gonna get to London after all. I've... just missed the last train.

TANNOY: 'The last train to London will be arriving at platform one in five minutes.'

DAFYDD LOOKS SHEEPISH. MYFANWY IS SYMPATHETIC.

MYFANWY: Bacardi and Coke?

DAFYDD: Yes please, Myfanwy.

THEY HOLD HANDS AND WALK OFF. WE SEE THE PAIR FROM BEHIND RETURNING TO THE VILLAGE, HOLDING HANDS.

DAFYDD: I'll go tomorrow.

MYFANWY: Yes, of course you will.

DAFYDD: (HANDING HIS CASE TO MYFANWY) Take that.

ANNE – CHRISTMAS DECORATIONS

INT: HOSPITAL/CORRIDOR.

TOM V/O: In Gash, just adjacent to the town of Coco Passage, is this hospital, run by Dr Lawrence.

DR LAWRENCE AND DR BEAGRIE ARE WALKING ALONG.

DR LAWRENCE: Well, we always celebrate Christmas here at the hospital and this year one of our patients, Anne, has very kindly offered to decorate the day room. I don't know if you've met Anne. Have you met Anne?

DR BEAGRIE NODS.

DR LAWRENCE: Well, it's just through here. Let's see how she's getting on.

INT: DAY ROOM. DR LAWRENCE AND DR BEAGRIE ENTER. THE FURNITURE HAS BEEN REARRANGED ERRATICALLY. SOME OF IT IS UPSIDE DOWN. WE SEE ANNE SMEARING 'MERY XMASS' ON THE WALLS IN WHAT LOOKS SUSPICIOUSLY LIKE EXCREMENT. DR BEAGRIE SNIFFS AND COVERS HIS MOUTH AND NOSE.

DR LAWRENCE: Hallo, Anne. How are you getting on?

ANNE: Eh-eh-eh.

DR LAWRENCE: Have you done the tree?

ANNE: Eh-eh-eh.

DR LAWRENCE: Ooh, what have you decorated it with?

ANNE WALKS THEM TO THE TREE. WE SEE THAT IT HAS BEEN DRESSED WITH DOZENS OF FISH FINGERS HANGING NEATLY, LIKE BAUBLES, FROM THE BRANCHES.

ANNE: Eh-eh-eh.

DR LAWRENCE: Fishfingers. That's... different. Well, thank you very much, Anne.

DR LAWRENCE AND DR BEAGRIE GO TO LEAVE. ANNE HOLDS UP SOME MISTLETOE.

ANNE: Eh-eh-eh.

DR LAWRENCE: (CHUCKLING) Oh, she's got some mistletoe. Do you want to kiss Dr Beagrie?

ANNE: (SHYLY) Eh-eh-eh.

DR LAWRENCE: (TO DR BEAGRIE) You don't mind, do you?

Don't you just love Christmas?

You've turned me bloody flat into a Thai bloody palace!

DR BEAGRIE GULPS AND SHAKES HIS HEAD, AS ANNE COMES TOWARDS HIM. SHE HOLDS THE MISTLETOE ABOVE HIS HEAD AND LICKS HIS ENTIRE FACE BEFORE PLANTING A KISS DELICATELY ON THE END OF HIS NOSE.

DR LAWRENCE: Don't you just love Christmas?

DUDLEY AND TING TONG – THAI PALACE

EXT: DUDLEY'S FLAT.

TOM V/O: It's approaching nightington and in Bruise, man Dudley Punt is on his way home.

DUDLEY AMBLES ALONG QUITE MERRILY WITH A PLASTIC BAG WITH A FEW BEER CANS IN.

DUDLEY: (SINGS TO HIMSELF IDLY) 'Happy talk, keep talkin' happy talk. Talk about things you'd like to do.'

HE APPROACHES THE FRONT DOOR, PUTS HIS KEY IN AND OPENS IT.

DUDLEY: Ting Tong? I'm home.

A YOUNG THAI MAN IN A BOW TIE AND WAISTCOAT MEETS A SURPRISED DUDLEY IN THE DOORWAY.

WAITER: Table for one, sir?

DUDLEY: What's going on?

THE WAITER LEADS A BAFFLED DUDLEY INTO THE LIVING ROOM, WHICH HAS BEEN DECORATED IN THE STYLE OF A THAI RESTAURANT. THERE IS THAI MUSIC PLAYING, A FEW WAITING STAFF AND VARIOUS PEOPLE DINING.

WAITER: Please. Take a seat please, sir.

THE WAITER HANDS DUDLEY A MENU WHICH READS 'TING TONG'S THAI PALACE'.

WAITER: I'm afraid we are out of Tom Yum soup.

DUDLEY: Where's Ting Tong? I wanna see Ting Tong.

WAITER: I think manageress is busy but I will check for you.

DUDLEY LOOKS BEMUSED. TING TONG APPEARS, IN UNIFORM.

TING TONG: Hello, Mr Dudley? I take it everything to your liking?

DUDLEY: No, it bloody isn't. You've turned me bloody flat into a Thai bloody palace!

TING TONG: Please, Mr Dudley. We do have other diners.

DUDLEY: I only nipped out to the offy.

A PASSING COUPLE HAVE PAID THEIR BILL AND GO TO LEAVE.

MAN: That was lovely, thank you very much.

TING TONG: No, thank you both. Please do come again, yes.

DUDLEY: No, don't come again! (TO TING TONG) Ting Tong Macadangdang, we need to talk.

TING TONG: I'm terribly sorry, Mr Dudley. We do have a bit of a crisis in the kitchen with the sticky rice balls. My brother here look after you.

TING TONG SIGNALS TO THE WAITER.

DUDLEY: Brother?

WAITER: The kitchen is about to close, sir. Are you ready to order?

DUDLEY: (FLUSTERED) I don't want anything!

The mints are for customers only.

WAITER: In that case, thank you very much, sir. Please come again soon.

THE WAITER POLITELY USHERS A BEMUSED DUDLEY TO THE DOOR. TING TONG'S MOTHER IS SEATED THERE DOING THE BOOKS. AT THE DOOR THERE IS A BOWL OF MINTS. DUDLEY GOES TO TAKE ONE.

WAITER: The mints are for customers only.

DUDLEY: Sorry.

WAITER: Thank you, sir.

DUDLEY IS SHOWN OUTSIDE. THE DOOR CLOSES. A HAND APPEARS IN THE WINDOW AND TURNS THE 'OPEN' SIGN TO 'CLOSED'. DUDLEY STANDS OUTSIDE HIS FLAT. HE PAUSES FOR A MOMENT BEFORE WANDERING OFF.

DUDLEY: (SINGS TO HIMSELF, SADLY) 'Happy talk, keep talking happy talk.'

MICHAEL AND SEBASTIAN – THE DEAL

EXT: NO 10 DOWNING STREET. A POLICEMAN STANDS GUARD. LOTS OF PRESS, FLASHBULBS ETC. MICHAEL IS STANDING OUTSIDE WITH SARAH AND SEBASTIAN.

TOM V/O: After a brief photocall with his wife...

PRESS: Go on, give him a kiss!

SARAH GOES TO KISS MICHAEL BUT IS BEATEN TO IT BY SEBASTIAN, WHO THEN REALISES THEY DIDN'T MEAN HIM. HE AFFECTS EMBARRASSMENT.

SEBASTIAN: Sorry, I thought you meant me – sorry.

TOM V/O: ...the Prime Minister has a long-overdue meeting with the Chancellor.

INT: PRIME MINISTER'S OFFICE. MICHAEL IS AT HIS DESK; SEBASTIAN SHOWS IN THE CHANCELLOR.

CHANCELLOR: So, the time has come.

MICHAEL: Yes, I know.

CHANCELLOR: We had a deal, Prime Minister.

MICHAEL: And I'll stick to it. I shall announce my resignation this afternoon, and the party will vote for the new leader on Thursday. You should be Prime Minister by the end of the week.

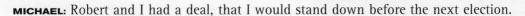

SEBASTIAN: (LOW) Wha-at?

MICHAEL: Robert and I had a deal, that I would stand down before the next election.

SEBASTIAN: Yeah, but you didn't mean it, did you?

MICHAEL: I gave him my word.

CHANCELLOR: I want the transition of power to run as smooth as possible. (TO SEBASTIAN) Sebastian, you will now work for me as the Prime Minister's aide.

SEBASTIAN: No thanks, I'm staying with Michael.

MICHAEL: I'm retiring from politics, I'm afraid, Sebastian. The new Prime Minister will be Robert.

SEBASTIAN: I don't like him.

MICHAEL: Why not?

SEBASTIAN: (SCREWS UP FACE) Well, he's all fat and Scottish.

CHANCELLOR: Very well, it looks like you'll be leaving government too, Sebastian. Prime Minister, I shall see you in the Commons at four.

MICHAEL: And I shall make my announcement then. Thank you, Robert.

MICHAEL: Sebastian, would you like to show the new Prime Minister out?

A MOPING SEBASTIAN SHOWS THE CHANCELLOR OUT.

MICHAEL: Thank you so much, Sebastian, for everything.

SEBASTIAN: (SHOCKED) So this is goodbye, then.

MICHAEL: I'm afraid so.

SEBASTIAN LOOKS MISTY-EYED. HE STARTS TO SNIFF.

EPISODE

MICHAEL: Sebastian, please don't cry.

SEBASTIAN: It's alright. I'm not going to.

SEBASTIAN IMMEDIATELY LETS OUT AN ENORMOUS WAIL AND BURSTS INTO FLOODS OF TEARS.

MICHAEL: Sebastian, please.

SEBASTIAN TALKS INCOMPREHENSIBLY THROUGH HIS TEARS FOR SOME TIME.

MICHAEL: I understand.

SEBASTIAN CONTINUES TO BAWL AND TALK INCOMPREHENSIBLY.

MICHAEL: Here.

MICHAEL HANDS SEBASTIAN A HANKY. SEBASTIAN BLOWS HIS NOSE.

SEBASTIAN: Can I keep this?

MICHAEL: Yes.

SEBASTIAN: (WEEPY) Whenever I have a good blow I'll think of you.

MICHAEL: Thank you, Sebastian. I wasn't going to give you this to you just yet but it seems like the right moment. I got it when I was at the summit last week in Switzerland.

MICHAEL GOES TO HIS DESK DRAW AND BRINGS OUT A SMALL BOX. HE HANDS IT TO SEBASTIAN. SEBASTIAN OPENS IT, STILL SNIFFLING. AND TAKES OUT AN EXPENSIVE-LOOKING SILVER WATCH.

SEBASTIAN: Thank you, it's beautiful.

SEBASTIAN STROKES MICHAEL'S FACE. FOR ONCE MICHAEL STANDS AND ENDURES IT.

MICHAEL: It's the least I can do, Sebastian.

SEBASTIAN: Actually, Prime Minister, I've got something for you.

Whenever I have a good blow I'll think of you.

MICHAEL: Really?

SEBASTIAN: (LOW VOICE) Yeah.

MICHAEL: But you didn't know I was leaving.

SEBASTIAN: (HUSKILY) Ssh. Close your eyes. It's a surprise.

MICHAEL DOES SO. WE REMAIN ON MICHAEL.

MICHAEL: Can I open them yet?

SEBASTIAN: (OOV) Yes.

WE SEE MICHAEL'S SHOCKED FACE. WE REVEAL THAT SEBASTIAN IS STANDING BEFORE MICHAEL, NAKED (WE SEE HIM FROM BEHIND). AT THAT MOMENT, THE PRIME MINISTER'S WIFE SARAH ENTERS. SHE IS INITIALLY OBLIVIOUS TO SEBASTIAN.

SARAH: Darling, do you want me to come with you to the press conferen—

SEBASTIAN: Sorry, we're in the middle of some important government business.

SARAH: Okay.

A STUNNED SARAH EXITS.

SEBASTIAN: Right. Where were we?

SEBASTIAN SHUFFLES FORWARD UNTIL HE IS UP CLOSE AND PERSONAL.

Right. Where were we?

LOU AND ANDY – MRS MEAD 4

EXT: CLIFF TOP. REMOTE, DESERTED AREA. MRS MEAD IS STANDING A FEW STEPS AHEAD OF ANDY.

ANDY: Can you push me?

MRS MEAD: No, no. You have to learn to wheel yourself. It's good exercise for you.

ANDY: I wanna go home.

MRS MEAD: Come on – it's only another two miles to go. I think that Lou has been far too soft on you.

MRS MEAD GOES TO TALK TO HIM UP CLOSE.

MRS MEAD: Oh yes, things are going to be different from now on. You've got into bad habits.

MRS MEAD SLAPS HIS CHEEK THEN TURNS TO GO AND LOOK OUT AT THE BEAUTIFUL SEA VIEW.

MRS MEAD: If you ask me I see no reason now why you can't do your own cooking and cleaning. And that TV is going off and staying off. And no more chocolate or potato crisps. And why don't get yourself a job? There's plenty of things you can do. First thing tomorrow I'm going to take you down the job centre and find something –

ANDY GETS OUT OF HIS CHAIR AND PUSHES HER OFF THE CLIFF. HE BRUSHES HIS HANDS TOGETHER – JOB DONE – GETS BACK INTO HIS CHAIR AND WHEELS HIMSELF IN THE DIRECTION HE CAME.

TOM V/O: And so another series of Little Britain comes to an end. A nation weeps. Why, even Her Majesty the Queen is said to be a fan. If you are watching, Queen, I hope you enjoyed the show, Ma'am, and, oh yes, next time you are opening Parliament why not pop one out? They look like beauties. Good, good.

INT: FLAT. ANDY SITS IN FRONT OF THE TELLY, MUNCHING AWAY ON REVELS. WE HEAR A KEY IN THE DOOR.

LOU: (OOV) Andy? It's Lou.

ANDY: Lou!

A BIG SMILE APPEARS ON ANDY'S FACE. EXCITEDLY HE GETS UP OUT OF HIS WHEELCHAIR TO GO AND WELCOME LOU BUT, REALISING WHAT HE'S DOING, HE QUICKLY RETURNS TO HIS CHAIR. ENTER LOU, WITH SUITCASE.

LOU: I'm home.

ANDY: (SHRUGS) Yeah, I know.

LOU LOOKS LIKE HE MIGHT GIVE ANDY A HUG BUT THINKS BETTER OF IT AND HEADS FOR THE KITCHEN.

LOU: I'll put your tea on.

A SMALL SMILE APPEARS ON ANDY'S FACE.

EPISODE

Little Britain series three

Written and performed
  by Matt Lucas and David Walliams
Director: Declan Lowney
Producer: Geoff Posner
Executive Producers: Myfanwy Moore,
  Jon Plowman
Script Editor: Richard Herring
Music: David Arnold
Location Manager: Thomas Howard
Location Assistant: Karen Smith
Sound: John Currie, Nick Robertson,
  Jem Whippey
Make Up and Hair Designer:
  Lisa Cavalli-Green
Make-up Assistants: Nicola Coleman,
  Suzi Munachen
Costume Designer: Annie Hardinge
Wardrobe Mistress: Sheena Gunn
Costume Assistant: Janine Marr,
  Aaron Timperly
Director of Photography: Katie Swain
Production Manager: Francis Gilson
Production Designer: Dennis de Groot
Production Buyer: Jac Hyman
Editor: Mykola Pawluk
Production Executive: Jez Nightingale
Script Supervisor: Chrissie Bibby
Production Co-Ordinator: Charlotte Lamb
Production Team: Sarah Hollingsworth,
  Harjeet Ghataora
Dubbing Mixer: Rob Butler-Biggs
1st Assistant Director: Andy Lumsden
Assistant Directors: Karen Howard,
  Angharad Jones, Stacy Crago
Art Director: Greg Shaw
Art Department: Daniel Ainslie,
  Simon Blackmoor, Brian Hampton,
  Rebecca Thompson, Nick Williamson,
  Rose Windsor
Casting: Tracey Gillham
Camera Team: David Penfold,
  Kirk Thornton, Bart Tuft, Ross Turley
Cameras: Nigel Saunders, John Sorapure
Studio Resource Manager: Andrew Garnett

Vision Mixer: Ros Storey
Visual Effects: Paul Fulton
Choreographer: Nicky Hinckley
Stage Manager: Caroline Caley
Floor Manager: Michael Matherson
Video Effects: Connan McStay.
Prop Master: Andrew Vining
Gaffer: Dominic Seal
Stunt Co-ordinator: Andreas Petrides
With thanks to Pozzitive Television
With the voice of Tom Baker
Special Guests: Rob Brydon, Anthony Head,
  Cat Deeley, Judy Finnigan, Nigel Havers,
  Richard Madeley, Derek Martin,
  David Baddiel, Ruth Madoc, Imelda Staunton

Featuring

Stephen Aintree, Keith Alexander, Mary Ann
Turner, Joanna Bacon, Sam Beazley, David
Benson, Su Bhoopongsa, Jiggy Bhore, Di
Botcher, Paul Charlton, Charubala Chokshi,
Sheila Collings, Joann Condon, Rebecca
Cooper, Naomi Cooper-Davis, Deddie Davies,
Patricia England, Cheryl Fergison, David
Foxxe, Richard Freeman, Steve Furst, Stirling
Gallacher, Kerry Gibson, Georgie Glen,
Georgie Glen, James Greene, Sally Hawkins,
Mike Hayward, Akiya Henry, Margaret Hilder,
Nazneen Hoseini, Margaret John, Ruth Jones,
Barabara Keogh, Ranjit Krishnama, Yuki
Kushida, Joshua Lawton, Phoenix Lee,
Freddie Lees, Geoff Leesley, Janette Legge,
Aimee Liddel, Steven Lim, Joan Linder, Alice
Lowe, Jennie Lucey, Damian Lynch, Elliot
Perry Mason, Diana May, Anita Mohan, Habib
Nasib Nader, Gordon Peters, Gregory Pitt, Paul
Putner, Kirris Riviere, Sally Rogers, Leelo Ross,
Danny Sapani, Shend , Harmage Singh,
Annelli Smith, Gordon Sterne, Mark Stobbart,
Margaret Towner, Menna Trussler, Carrigan
Van Der Merwe, Indira Varma, Eleanor Vickers,
Matthew Ward, Dean Whatton.

Matt and David would also like to thank Conor McCaughan, Melanie
Rockcliffe, Barbara Charone, Moira Bellas and all at HarperCollins.

**The complete Series 1, 2 and 3 are also available on DVD, and the
original Radio 4 series are available on BBC Audio CD and cassette and
in a special tin gift set with bonus discs.**